Advance Praise for *Compassion*

"Ilia Delio leads us on our quest for an authentic inner compass, challenging us to action and to be 'doers of the Word.'"
—Margaret Carney, O.S.F., president, St. Bonaventure University

"For today's reader, tired of relationships based on texting and virtual reality, here is a strong voice for a person-to-person encounter with the suffering neighbor awaiting her Samaritan."
—William J. Short, O.F.M., dean, Franciscan School of Theology, Berkeley

"Ilia Delio's insights about the spirituality of space represent just a part of her unique understanding of the kind of compassion so needed in our world today."
—Michael H. Crosby, O.F.M. CAP., author, *Thank God Ahead of Time: The Life and Spirituality of Solanus Casey*

COMPASSION

Other works by Ilia Delio, o.s.f.

Crucified Love: Bonaventure's Mysticism of the Crucified Christ

Simply Bonaventure: An Introduction to His Life, Thought, and Writings

A Franciscan View of Creation: Learning to Live in a Sacramental World

Franciscan Prayer

Clare of Assisi: A Heart Full of Love

The Humility of God: A Franciscan Perspective

Care for Creation: A Franciscan Spirituality of the Earth
(with Keith Douglass Warner, o.f.m., and Pamela Wood)

Ten Evenings with God

Christ in Evolution

The Emergent Christ: Exploring the Meaning of Catholic in an Evolutionary Universe

compassion

Living in the Spirit of St. Francis

I<small>LIA</small> D<small>ELIO</small>, o.s.f.

franciscan
media
Cincinnati, Ohio

Permission to publish excerpts from *Francis of Assisi: Early Documents* granted by New City Press, New York.

Cover design by Candle Light Studios
Cover image © Shutterstock | Jill Battaglia
Book design by Mark Sullivan

LIBRARY OF CONGRESS CATALOGING-IN-PUBLICATION DATA
Delio, Ilia.
Compassion : living in the spirit of Francis of Assisi / Ilia Delio.
p. cm.
Includes bibliographical references.
ISBN 978-1-61636-162-4 (alk. paper)
1. Compassion—Religious aspects—Christianity. 2. Francis, of Assisi, Saint, 1182-1226. I. Title.
BV4647.S9D45 2011
241'.4—dc23
2011023338

Published by Franciscan Media
28 W. Liberty St.
Cincinnati, OH 45202
www.FranciscanMedia.org

Go alone and away from all books,
go with your own heart into the storm of human hearts
and see if somewhere in that storm
there are bleeding hearts...

—CARL SANDBURG,
"Good Morning, America"

CONTENTS

| ACKNOWLEDGMENTS |

| I am deeply grateful to my former student, Fr. Harry Monaco, O.F.M., for his gracious assistance with this book. His willingness to help in the midst of his battle with cancer was truly admirable. Harry contributed to the first half of the book when the power of chemotherapy consumed his energy. Compassion was not an idea for Harry but a living reality. He told me of the many blessings he received from the staff of the hospital where he lay for several weeks. He experienced compassion in different colors, cultures, religions, and professions, and what amazed Harry was that every compassionate person spoke the same language of love.

To Harry and all those struggling with illness, I dedicate this book.

| I am sitting in the Denver International Airport sipping coffee at a McDonald's located in one of the main terminal squares. I am pondering the meaning of compassion as I watch numerous people pass by, each with a destination privy only to a few, if anyone at all. I am awed by the human face, each one unique and expressive, each person belonging to someone and to something. The human person is a mini-universe, each with his or her own Big Bang history walking into a future created simply by being alive. But strangely, no one is looking at anyone else, or if they are, like me, they are doing so stealthily so as not to be noticed.

The prevalence of anonymity marks our culture today; hence the desire for some people to be identified either by dress, tattoos, or sculptured hair. We are wired together on the Internet, on our Droids, iPhones, and video screens, but face to face we are like marble statues. What keeps us together and apart simultaneously? Why do we fear being humanly related to one another? I am sitting at McDonald's fully aware of this corporation's participation in the industrialization of food and its use of synthetic elements to create consumer food products. McDonald's typifies the radical disconnect in the food economy; humans disconnected from the economy of food are humans disconnected from the economy of life.

It is late and shops are beginning to close as the flights take off for their destinations. My flight has been cancelled so I have the privilege of time, watching the airport workers arrive on their night shifts to clean the terminals, the carpets and chairs occupied by the millions of people who have passed through the airport this day. The workers are not white Anglo Saxons but foreign born. They arrive around midnight and will work until the sun begins to rise. Had my flight not been cancelled I would not have known of this world of the airport worker. We live in such private worlds with private concerns and private dreams, it is no wonder we fear the immigrant and stranger intruding on our private property. We hardly know our neighbor's struggles and sometimes we barely know our own.

There is much talk these days about immigration and welcoming the stranger into our midst. We fear what will happen to our families and communities if we allow too many strangers into our comfortable lives, insensitive at times to the fact that they too are seeking food, family, and friends. The evangelist John wrote "there is no fear in love, but perfect love cast out fear" (1 John 4:18). Love transforms, the medievalists said, because love unites. Love seeks the good of the other. Compassion is the feeling of love that rends the veil of the stranger and unites one human to another, heart to heart.

The Jesuit mystic Pierre Teilhard de Chardin described the human species in evolution toward the fullness of unity in love. He was concerned about the increasing pressures of human life due to overpopulation, war, and human conflict, and saw that humanity was becoming increasingly fragmented. In his view, neither escapism nor existential despair can further the evolutionary process. Rather, the way forward is a new spirituality by which humans around the globe can unite to become one mind and one heart in love, a new *ultrahumanity* united in love.

Compassion is a thread that binds together the deepest centers of life beyond the borders of race, gender, religion, tribe, or creature. Donald McNeill and others write:

> The word *compassion* is derived from the Latin words *pati* and *cum*, which together mean "to suffer with." Compassion asks us to go where it hurts, to enter into places of pain, to share in brokenness, fear, confusion, and anguish. Compassion challenges us to cry out with those in misery, to mourn with those who are lonely, to weep with those in tears. Compassion requires us to be weak with the weak, vulnerable with the vulnerable, and powerless with the powerless. Compassion means full immersion in the condition of being human.[1]

We are at a critical threshold today in our earthly life where we either must overcome our fears and evolve to a new level of love, or undergo the slow death that underlies fragmentation. What will unite this earthly community? What will join human hearts together despite our different colors, languages, cultures, and religions?

Compassion is the river that overflows into the ocean of love that has no end; it crosses all borders to embrace the suffering of another. Here I think we can learn from Francis of Assisi, that great medieval saint who, in his own time, broke down the barriers between rich and poor and made the love of God available to all.

The key to Francis' transformation into love, his secret of making wholes out of the scattered fragments of life, was compassion. He learned compassion as the art of healing broken hearts by collecting the tears of the forgotten, the frightened, and the lonely in his hands and holding the wounded as his kin. Francis entered the world of the stranger and made the stranger into a brother. He learned to love what was weak and fragile, and he learned to care for what the world discarded.

As I watch individual persons scurry around the airport looking for spouses, holding on to their children, with their eyes looking intently at terminal signs and flight schedules, I think our greatest fear is our deepest desire: to love and to be loved. We long to be for another and to give ourselves nobly to another, but we fear the cost of love. Deep within we yearn for wholeness in love, but to become more whole in love we must accept our weaknesses and transcend our limits of separation in order to unite in love. We long for oneness of heart, mind and soul, but we fear the demands of unity. Sometimes I think we choose to be alone because it is safe. To be comfortable in our isolation is our greatest poverty.

Compassion transcends isolation because the choice to be for another is the rejection of being alone. The compassionate person recognizes the other as part of oneself in a way that is mystical and ineffable. It is not a rational caring for another but a deep identification with the other as brother and sister. Francis was recognized as a new Christ through his gift of compassion. He exchanged his private, comfortable life for the life of a poor brother, seeing in the suffering of others something of his own life.

What is compassion and how does it emerge in the human heart? What moves one to compassion? Can we learn compassion as a way of life? Can we let go of our fears to love more deeply? These are some of the questions that guide this little book on compassion pondered in an airport. It is not meant to be a great study or a comprehensive analysis of a virtue but an exploration into what expands the human heart for another—ultimately what unites.

CHAPTER ONE

The Marketplace of Exchange

| The Bernardone family to which Francis belonged was part of the rising merchant class in the medieval town of Assisi. His father was a cloth merchant and owned a shop in Assisi where Francis worked for some time. He was not only familiar with the daily business of buying and trading cloth, but he came into contact with many different types of people—farmers, craftsmen, artists, bakers—people who worked with their hands and valued the material things of the earth. He regarded earthly life as possessing ideal, positive potential as God's creation. Some regard him as "the first materialist" in the best sense of the word because of the way he looked on the material world—not for *what* it is but for *how* it is—God's creation.[1]

The first biographer of Francis, Thomas of Celano, describes him as a vain young man: "Maliciously *advancing beyond* all of his *peers* in vanities, he proved himself a more excessive *inciter of evil and a zealous imitator* of foolishness. He was an object of admiration to all, and he endeavored to surpass others in his flamboyant display of vain accomplishments: wit, curiosity, practical jokes and foolish talk, songs and soft flowing garments."[2] Francis' wealth, according to Celano, made him "not greedy but extravagant, not a hoarder of money but a squanderer of property" and he would strut about the narrow streets of Assisi with his band of followers who enjoyed the flamboyant merchant.

Despite his material comforts and circle of friends, Francis was not at peace with himself or the world around him. Francis was ambitious for glory and fame and although he was not from the noble class, he sought to achieve these by becoming a knight—something quite inaccessible to him, yet something that he desired, nevertheless.

His aspiration for knighthood was all bound up in a desire to buy his way into another societal class. The knight represented a certain kind of "model" that Francis was trying to imitate—much different from the model of Christ—who he would eventually come to imitate in place of the knight. Knighthood is not associated with compassion, but with honor—honor which is gained as a result of fierce competition. Francis not only experienced a defeat in this competition, he was also seriously wounded. Seeking to accomplish a great victory, Francis lost the battle.

As he lay wounded in a soldier's hospital, Francis experienced the nearness of death and began to wonder about the direction of his life. His serious illness caused a profound change within him. Thomas of Celano describes this change in terms of divine "punishment," but I think we can reframe this in terms of a "wake-up call."

Through his illness Francis began to realize the limitations of his body. Anyone who has experienced illness can likely relate to Francis' awareness of his bodily limits. Prayer can help us see the hand of God at work in using illness—and the frailties of our *bodies*—as a way to alert us to the deeper realities of our life. It is not so much that God directly causes the illness or wills it upon us, but God uses the darkness of illness to enlighten within us a new vision of reality. The medieval use of the word "punishment" can distract us from the deeper truth; that we must "wake up" to what is most important in life. Thomas writes:

> Thus worn down by long illness, as human obstinacy deserves since it is rarely remedied except through punishment, he began *to mull over within himself* things that were not usual for him. When he had recovered a little and, with the support of a cane, had begun to walk about here and there through the house in order to regain his health, he went outside one day and began to gaze on the surrounding countryside with greater interest. But the beauty of the fields, the delight of the vineyards, and whatever else was beautiful to see could offer him no delight at all. He wondered at the sudden change in himself, and considered those who loved these things quite foolish.[3]

This is the same Francis who would eventually compose the "Canticle of the Creatures," the song of family with all creation. One of the earliest steps toward writing that masterpiece occurs here, after his illness, when he goes out and gazes on the countryside with a deeper interest. He starts to notice things that he did not notice before; yet, at this early stage, he experiences "no delight at all." What does this mean?

Perhaps it represents a vague awareness that his life had been alienated from the earth around him, but he was not aware of this disconnectedness. Thomas indicates that Francis himself was in the process of conversion—or, dare we say—"evolution," a transitional space where his "past and present transgressions no longer delighted him,

[but] he was not yet fully confident of refraining from future ones."[4] In our own lives, when we experience loss or illness, we are confronted with a choice to either see it as an interruption or impediment to our comfortable lives or an invitation to go deeper into our relationship with God, cultivating a sense of compassion for others around us who also experience loss or illness. We are also invited to develop compassion for our natural world, which suffers from the fatal wounds of war and human indifference.

As Francis' life changed, he began to pray and to sense the presence of God deep within him. When he recovered from his injuries, he returned to Assisi with the desire for a new direction in life. He started wandering about in broken-down churches and would spend long periods of time praying in these places. He began to discover the value of time and space. As a merchant seller in Assisi, he had no time for the poor and the lepers, only for the enjoyment of his friends.

The injuries of battle slowed him down, however, confining him to a bed, and there he began to discover the value of prayer. When he recovered and returned home, he did not return to the frenetic pace of a cloth merchant but the slowed time of one who is injured. Physically healed, Francis' soul was in need of healing, and he began to look for his soul amid the ruins of churches.

One day he wandered into the broken-down church of San Damiano, located outside the gates of Assisi. As he did, he saw a large, Byzantine icon of the crucified Christ, pierced but light filled, bleeding but not dripping blood. Rather, blood bursts forth from Jesus' wounds, as if quenching the thirst of the community of disciples gathered around him.

As he prayed quietly before this cross, Francis was grasped by an overwhelming experience of divine love. He felt deeply embraced by

God's compassionate love, and he wept, knowing his own brokenness. He heard a voice coming from the cross saying, "Francis, go rebuild my house, as you see, it is all being destroyed."[5] He understood this to mean at first the house of the actual church, and so he gathered stones so that he could rebuild the structure. The real church to be rebuilt, however, was not the stone church but the temple of his soul. It is much easier to build a house than to build a soul, but Francis understood that without a living soul, there is no house to worship God. And so, a new direction for his life was set.

A Change in Consciousness

Conversion is the grace of letting go and turning in the dance of life. It is awakening to the fact that old habits must die for new vision to be born. The classic story told of Francis' conversion is his meeting of the leper. It was well known that Francis abhorred lepers; however, one day (shortly after his conversion) he met a leper along the way in his travels. Instead of running away from the leper, Francis stopped, dismounted his horse, gave the leper alms, and kissed the leper's ulcerous hand. It was an outrageous act completely contrary to Francis' personality; yet he tells us in his "Testament" (written at the end of his life) that in the kiss of the leper's hand, "what had seemed bitter to me was turned into sweetness of soul and body." [6] Overcoming his revulsion of lepers and putting aside his own animosity, Francis experienced the goodness of God in the weak, disfigured flesh of the leper.

The story continues that after kissing the leper's hand, Francis mounted his horse to ride on. As he began to ride, he turned back to see the leper, but there was no leper in sight. Some scholars have interpreted this to mean that Francis had to come to terms with his own inner lepers, to heal the wounds within him in his long journey to wholeness.

Once the party boy of Assisi, Francis now wandered into solitary places—mountains and ravines—where he would water the ground with his prayers and tears. The narrow streets of Assisi and the bustle of the marketplace could not give Francis the space he needed to attend to the intimate presence of God.

There is an important connection between place, space, and grace that gives birth to compassion in the life of Francis. For the divine and human to meet, the place of encounter needs space. Francis sought the space of the wilderness to hear the sounds of the intimate presence of God. In her poem "The Fire Within The Fire of All Things," Catherine de Vinck captures this return to the wilderness as the discovery of the divine:

> I start here
>   in the mud of the rainy season
> —the land's ragged fabric
>   coarse under the probing hand:
> brittle sedge, lifeless vine
>   thorny twig of the vanished rose...
>   ...
> if I dance with happiness
>   at the sight of the circling hawk
> knowing for a moment what it is
>   to float over the swamp
>   in a robe of dark feathers;
> and if I do hear the summons
>   hidden within the miracle of stones:
> then I can name the holy
>   the Fire within the fire of all things.[7]

Science, Space, and Time

The wilderness alters our experience of time. It slows us down and merges us with the wonder of creation's wild beauty. Time unveils the wonders of space, and space-time reveals the face of God. Modern science has been exploring the dimensions of space-time since Albert Einstein's groundbreaking theory of relativity. The mathematician Sir Isaac Newton thought that space was absolute, like a container for matter. But Einstein showed that space and time are integral dimensions of the universe, affected by gravity or the weight of matter and energy which comprise the universe.

Space-time seems to have a hidden relationship with consciousness. Pierre Teilhard de Chardin said that the whole process of evolution is an unfolding of consciousness, as matter becomes spirit. From the Big Bang onward, consciousness is part of the material world, the "withinness" according to Teilhard, of the material "withoutness." The symmetry between light and consciousness evokes the idea that mind is in matter. Astrophysicist James Jeans writes: "The universe begins to look more like a great thought than a great machine. Mind no longer appears as an accidental intruder into the realm of matter; we are beginning to suspect that we ought rather to hail it as the creator and governor of the realm of matter...."[8] The mindfulness of the universe suggested by quantum physics may be the equivalent of what the Greeks described as *Logos*.

If consciousness is a dimension of light, and light is the measurement of time and space, then we can see a relationship between consciousness, time, and space. If consciousness shrinks and is disconnected from the surrounding environment, then space shrinks as well. The narrowing of consciousness and space is the narrowing of time. As time shortens, one tries desperately to get out of the space one is confined in.

7

In a sense, this is what happened to Francis. He experienced a change in consciousness, and he sought new space by leaving his familiar surroundings of Assisi, wandering into the hills of central Italy and entering into abandoned churches to pray. Francis left Assisi not only to pray but to enter a deeper space of relatedness which he experienced within his soul. He became conscious of how money and greed fracture relationships between people. Assisi had become a market economy driven by profit, and Francis renounced the shift from a gift economy, driven by direct relationships with others in which money played no part, to this new economy, which was driven by money and which minimized the significance of human relationships.[9] Profit and greed monetized relationships and excluded those who were poor.

As someone caught up in the market economy, Francis had to come to terms with his own exclusion of the poor through the pursuit of money. His illness helped him realize the inestimable value of the human person, and prayer helped him realize the value of his own life in God.

Prayer changes us because it is that deep dialogue with God who is the source of our lives. To pray is to be at home with oneself in the presence of God. It is taking hold of one's life with its flaws, weaknesses, and dreams, and sharing these with God.

Many of the saints recognized that we know ourselves better in God than in ourselves, because the self created by God is known best by God. Prayer is becoming conscious of our inner self as the self that belongs to God. Thomas of Celano wrote that Francis "would direct all his attention and affection / toward the *one thing* he *asked of the Lord*, / not so much praying as becoming totally prayer."[10] To become living prayer is to enter a new place of refuge in God, a place of union in love. It is to be at home in the cosmos which, Sally McFague said, is the body of God.[11] To enter the heart of God is to enter into a new space and a new relatedness to the world. Time takes on a new dimension because life in God is infinite. As prayer gives birth to the new inner universe, the soul expands in love.

Francis trusted the voice of God he heard speaking from the San Damiano cross—"go, rebuild my house"—and he trusted the Spirit of love that embraced him deep within. He trusted enough to let go of the comfortable life he enjoyed in Assisi to enter into the unknown love of the God of the universe. Did he fear for his life? Thomas of Celano recounts a story of Francis praying in darkness. As he prayed he saw a vision of an old hunchbacked woman, ugly and decrepit. He perceived the presence of the Evil One telling him that if he continued praying he would end up looking like this woman. Trusting in the power of love over fear, Francis continued praying and the vision disappeared.[12] Peace settled like morning dew on the fresh grass of his fragile inner life. Love has the power to triumph over evil because love is the power of God.

Thomas realized a deep movement in Francis born in his encounter with the leper. Francis had profound disgust for lepers during his youth and would quickly run away at the sight of a leper. After he recovered from his illness, he began to pray more earnestly. One day he met a leper and instead of running away, he approached the leper and kissed the disfigured hand and gave the leper alms. Francis' encounter with the leper was inextricably linked with the voice of God he heard from the cross. In his "Remembrance of the Desire of a Soul," Thomas of Celano draws the link between Francis' encounter with lepers and his experience at San Damiano. He describes Francis' disdain of lepers and his horror on seeing them or passing them on the road. One day, around the time of Francis' conversion, Francis was traveling and met a leper on the road. While he was at first repulsed by the sight of the disfigured human, he did not want to dishonor God and so he dismounted his horse and went to meet the leper. When the leper stretched out his hand for money, Francis kissed his hand and gave him alms. The leper was surprised by Francis' act but graciously accepted the alms. Francis mounted his horse and departed from the leper. He rode a short distance and then turned back to see the leper once again; however, the leper had disappeared. The event touched Francis deeply. He found where the lepers lived and went to visit them, giving them alms and kissing them. The eyes of Francis were opened to see the lepers' goodness. What had been disdainful became desirable; the bitter became sweet. After describing Francis' encounter with the leper, Thomas of Celano describes Francis' encounter with God in the crucified Christ. This sequence of events is not coincidental but a theological interpretation. Whereas we might assume that Francis moved from God to the human person, Thomas indicates that the leper was the starting point for Francis' experience of God. This experience culminates in his encounter with the crucified Christ. Thomas writes:

> With his heart already completely changed—soon his body was also to be changed—he was walking one day by the church of San Damiano, which was abandoned by everyone and almost in ruins. *Led by the Spirit* he went in to pray and knelt down devoutly before the crucifix. He was shaken by unusual experiences and discovered that he was different from when he had entered. As soon as he had this feeling, there occurred *something unheard of in previous ages*: with the lips of the painting, the image of the Christ crucified spoke

to him. "Francis," it said, *calling him by name,* "go rebuild My house; as you see, it is all being destroyed". . . . . From that time on, compassion for the Crucified was impressed into his holy soul. And we honestly believe the wounds of the sacred Passion were impressed deep in his heart, though not yet in his flesh.[13]

It is significant that the voice of the crucified Christ spoke to Francis shortly after his encounter with the voiceless leper, who in the account by Celano, disappeared on the roadside. The noted anthropologist René Girard describes the scapegoat mechanism which involves the disappearance and silence of the scapegoated victim, the innocent one who bears the violence intended for the enemy. The victim's true identity is concealed or veiled from view. In Celano's account, the disappearance of the leper appears as a literary technique to alert the reader that this is no ordinary leper—it is Christ. On another level, however, Celano does not allow the leper to disappear permanently. Francis needs to consciously acknowledge the truth of the person that he saw. Three days after his encounter with the leper, he "made his way to the houses of the lepers." The "house" of lepers represents a foreshadowing of the "house" of Christ which Francis will hear about in the church of San Damiano. The veil which covered and rendered silent the true identity of the leper was irrevocably lifted for Francis when he heard the San Damiano cross speak.

The story of Francis among the lepers is a story of death and resurrection. In his "Testament," Francis says: "[W]hen I was in sin, it seemed bitter for me to see lepers. And the Lord himself led me among them and *I showed mercy* to them. And when I left them, what had seemed bitter to me was turned into sweetness of soul and body."[14] The relationship between sin, grace, and life in Francis' encounter with the leper reminds us of the resurrection narratives where the disciples do not immediately recognize the identity of Jesus; they are blinded by their own concerns. Mary Magdalene, for example, "turned around and saw Jesus standing there, but she did not know that it was Jesus" (John 20:14). For the disciples on the road to Emmaus, the recognition of Jesus came after he has disappeared from their midst: "Were not our hearts burning within us while he was talking to us on the road, while he was opening the scriptures to us?" (Luke 24:32).

These resurrection stories, like the story of Francis and the leper, show us that conversion involves a movement from nonrecognition to recognition; we are invited to see the hidden presence of God. Something took place in Francis' encounter with the leper that was a resurrection experience. Francis met the leper and then heard the voice from the crucifix. His movement of conversion was not from God to humanity but from humanity to God; in kissing the fragile disfigured flesh of the leper, Francis heard the voice of Christ. The voice of the San Damiano cross was the voice of Christ and the leper, one and the same voice, because the leper—the scapegoated victim of Assisi's society—had been rendered virtually silent by a ritual of death. Now risen from the tomb, the leper was no longer rendered to the silent realm of death, but given an irrevocable voice. Francis heard the voice of truth in this encounter and from this point forward "compassion for the Crucified was impressed into his holy soul."[15] After this moment, there would be no turning back—the truth had been revealed to Francis and was written on his heart. He would always hear the voice of this leper because he heard the truth of Christ's Passion, liberating the voice of the voiceless. In Christ all share in the freedom of the children of God.

Meditation

To become living prayer is to enter a new place of refuge in God.

For Reflection

In his "Testament" Francis writes:

> The Lord gave me, Brother Francis, thus to begin doing penance in this way: for when I was in sin, it seemed too bitter for me to see lepers. And the Lord Himself led me among them and *I showed mercy* to them. And when I left them, what had seemed bitter to me was turned into sweetness of soul and body. And afterwards I delayed a little and left the world.[16]

1. Can you think of a time in your own life when you experienced something similar to Francis' experience, for example, when you experienced something "bitter" being turned into "sweetness of soul and body"?

2. In the context of this short passage, what do you think Francis means by "doing penance"? What are the characteristics of "doing penance"?

3. What do you think Francis means when he says he "left the world"? What "world" did he leave behind?

4. Reflect on the persons you reject. Pray for them. What are some ways you can return to them?

CHAPTER TWO

The Wilderness of the Heart

| The heart can be a lonely, wild place. Deep within, like a cavernous well, the heart is the place of cosmic birth and oneness with the mystery of life. The heart is the sacred inner space where divine and human tightly bond in a still point of utter silence. It is well known that Francis prayed before the San Damiano crucifix for inner light of his heart:

> Most High
> Glorious God,
>   enlighten the darkness of my heart
>   and give me
>   true faith, certain hope,
>   and perfect charity,
>   sense and knowledge,
> Lord,
>   that I may carry out
> Your holy and true command.[1]

This is a striking prayer because as Francis prayed before the crucified Christ he experienced the Most High God. Franciscan scholar

Michael Blastic writes: "...[I]t is the life of Jesus in its very fragile humanity that is salvific."[2] Fragile humanity and Most High God are bound together as one without confusion, separation or division. Francis sought to be at home with God in weak, fragile humanity, and the way to know this hidden God is through the heart.

For too long we have made God an object of our desire, hope, frustration, and anger. But God is not an object outside ourselves onto which we can project what is within ourselves. Rather God is within us, our deepest self, as St. Augustine wrote: "[Y]ou were more inward than my inmost self, and superior to my highest being."[3] Because God is, I am. Yet, God is not limited to me. Rather, God is the infinite fecund source of all that exists. To know God is to know the world as it truly is in the depth of reality. Francis realized that he could not know truth until he could see clearly the light of truth, and true vision is possible with the eyes of the heart.

The heart is a wild place, however, because it is filled with the deepest truth of who we are and thus with the little secrets of our lives. We are constantly trying to control our hearts so that our secrets will not be revealed; in doing so, however, our vision of truth is always blurred. In our pragmatic, scientific culture, we do not deal well with unruly nature; we must wrest wildness from nature and control it by force and manipulation. We fear rebellion of the wild, as if the unknown may rise up and conquer us by surprise. Little do we know that wildness is the most apt description of reality. God is wild love.

We are losing the sense of wilderness today. Technology promises to control the wild and create a controlled, manageable life. Richard Louv's book, *Last Child in the Woods*, describes the modern child as having nature deficit disorder. Glued in front of a light-emitting diode screen, today's child discovers the wilderness more in cyberspace than in nature space. Online wilderness is not really wild at all. One click of the mouse can shift the view of nature's wilderness to Pokemon or solitaire or Facebook. Children are no longer left free to play in nature and to let nature play.

Without play the human imagination to dream and create is stifled; spontaneity is mutated to short bits of controlled information. The Jesuit mystic Pierre Teilhard de Chardin spent long periods of time in the desert and came to see the value of the wilderness in the formation of the human person. Teilhard indicated that to be fully human we must get away from what is "merely human" and return to the wilderness. He called us to leave the cities and find the unexplored wilderness by returning to matter, to find ourselves where the soul is most deep and where matter is most dense; to feel the *plenitude* of our powers of action and adoration effortlessly ordered within our deepest selves.[4]

This notion of "returning" to matter is very significant. Our contemporary aversion to wilderness and to "matter" is essentially a modern form of a very ancient heresy: namely, gnosticism, the belief that God did not truly enter into union with our humanity and that knowledge alone will save us. Conversion involves doing what Christ did, that is, becoming human again—returning to *humus* or the earth/clay from which we were created.

Christ is the New Adam—and it is no accident that the word *Adam* literally means "clay" in Hebrew. It also means "red" and "blood." Christ is the "God-man." The fourth-century Cappadocian father, St. Basil of Caesarea, wrote: "The human being is an animal who has the received the vocation to become God."[5]

But before we can make this journey to becoming God, we must embrace our humanity as Christ did. Irenaeus of Lyons addresses a question to Adam and Eve in the Garden of Eden which captures this: "How could you be God when you have not yet become human? How could you be complete when you have only just been created?"⁶ Francis had his own version of this when he prays in his "Office of the Passion": "Take up your bodies, and *carry* his holy cross."⁷ Bearing the weaknesses of our bodies is the path to resurrection and anything that denies or annihilates the body annihilates the Resurrection as well.

The medieval person did not have an extended self in cyberspace, like the twenty-first-century person. Rather, the medieval person sought God by going away from the busy world to remote places to pray, meditate, and reflect on the deeper meaning of life. Pilgrimages were popular in the Middle Ages. Francis went into solitary woods and forests in order to enter the wilderness of his heart. He prayed, entering the darkness of his heart, unafraid to ask for grace: "Ask and it will be given to you; search, and you will find; knock, and the door will be opened for you" (Luke 11:9).

To ask is to acknowledge that one does not know or possess; it is to admit dependency on another. We fail to ask when we refuse to be dependent; we assume self-sufficiency and thus we limit ourselves and the possibilities within us for something more than ourselves. To ask in prayer is to acknowledge the limits of our humanity. God is like a beggar waiting at the soul's door, Vladimir Lossky wrote, not daring to force it open. God creates us out of love and thus bestows true freedom. "God becomes *powerless* before human freedom."⁸

If divine love was not free, we could not *choose* to love, and if we could not *choose* to love, then we would not be free. Hence God does not force, control or manipulate our destinies. Rather, God allows us to be, and in the freedom of our creation, God is ever faithful love. As Beloved, God strengthens and supports us, inviting us into relationship without forcing us but never giving up on us, always faithful and always desirous that we will respond in love.

There is a passage from *The Color Purple* that captures this sense of God's longing for us and God dwelling in us. It is a dialogue between Shug and Celie, two friends who are African American women trying to make sense of a world of intense suffering. The passage is in the context of a letter that Celie is writing to her sister Nettie. Shug tells Celie that God is not some*thing* but God is everything that is or ever was or ever will be. We are always looking *for* God, but we "come into the world with God," she says, and therefore the only way to find God is to look inside where God lives. Only those who search for God inwardly find God. Celie questions Shug about God's gender because she has grown up thinking God is an old white man, but Shug says that God is neither male nor female but beyond gender. God is everything that exists; and because God is in everything, we can feel God, if we awaken to God's presence. She tells Celie that one day she was sitting quietly, feeling forlorn "like a motherless child" when it dawned on her that she was part of everything, the trees, the birds, the air, because God lived in her and in everything else. This was a moment of revelation for Shug and she tells Celie how she *knew* that she had experienced God. Shug realized that God is not the "great big man" sitting upstairs in heaven watching us to see if we get things right. God is really other than what we imagine God to be because God lives in ordinary persons and trees and skies and creatures. God is the stranger in our midst who we do not recognize. We are always trying to please God, but it is God who is always trying to please us. God is always surprising us with gifts of grace when we least expect them. We talk and talk about God, Shug tells Celie, but somehow we cannot get that "old white man" out of our heads. We are so busy thinking about God or talking about God that we never notice anything God makes, not a tree or a blade of grass or a wildflower.[9] The Islamic sage Ibn ʾArabi spoke of God's presence in the mystical language of love: "I have called you so often and you have not heard me. I have shown myself to you so often and you have not seen me. I have made myself fragrant so often, and you have not smelled me."[10] In her own simple way, Shug too reached the heart of the mystical God who is so near to our touch and deep within our lives that we cannot believe that *this* is God. The Dominican mystic Meister Eckhart prayed to be rid of God so that he could really live in God. Dionysius said that the primary name of God is silence. To know God is to love life and to let life enter within us. God is hidden in what is weak and fragile and too much God talk can easily ignore the divine presence. God is the "more" of what we seek.

The God of the mystics is not the God of the philosophers, not the God who sits in heaven watching over creation in judgment. Rather it is the hidden God who pours out his love for the beloved, a God who lets go of being God to be God for us. Being in relationship with this God of outpouring love does not insulate us from destruction or calamity. We are not exempt from the sufferings of life. On the contrary, the one who enters into the wild love of God—for divine love is not neat, logical, and orderly—enters in the unknown forces of the heart. Deep within us God dwells as fire, turbulent wind, a raging ocean of power and yet a deep silence of stillness. God is all of these because divine love is dynamic, active, generative, infinite, and good. God is the fullness of everything that lives, moves, and has being. To enter the human heart is to enter into God unafraid to risk the unknown or death itself, since "love is stronger than death." God's weakness in love enkindles the strength of humanity. "Resurrection,"

Richard Kearney writes, "returns us to the world so that we may live more abundantly."[11]

Francis spent long periods of time in the wilderness. "When praying in the woods or solitary places he would fill the forest with groans," and "water the places with tears,"[12] calling upon God and asking for light on the unknown path of his journey. From his first encounter with Christ Crucified at San Damiano, Francis knew that the path of love is one of suffering, not just physical suffering but that deep suffering of change whereby one becomes a stranger to the once familiar family and friends. Thomas of Celano said that Francis wept "loudly over the Passion of Christ, as if it was constantly before his eyes. He filled the roads with his sobbing, and, as he remembered the wounds of Christ, he would take no comfort."[13]

Francis was very much like the desert fathers and mothers who left the familiar surroundings of home to enter into the wilderness of nature to encounter truth. The life of St. Antony, for example, tells of a young man from a prosperous family who heard the Gospel call— "go sell what you possess and give to the poor"—the same Gospel that spoke to Francis. Disposing of his wealth, Antony began to live a life of discipline by practicing prayer and poverty under the direction of an older hermit. After some time, Antony withdrew completely to the desert where he encountered a succession of temptations and battled with the demons in solitude. In the desert Antony redefined the ascetic as one who fought the adversary face to face. It is said that he made the "desert a city" by sanctifying a place where God had not been present. However, he did not stay in the desert but returned from solitude after about twenty years to act as a spiritual father to those seeking true Christian life.

While Francis' life could be likened to the desert fathers, his was more closely related to the Syrian ascetical movement which differed from the eremitical movement of the Egyptian desert. Syrian asceticism involved both men and women and was a choice of life made as an adult at baptism. The ascetic was a solitary, a single-minded one, who sought discipleship as a literal imitation of the poor, homeless, and celibate Jesus. The wandering life of the Syrian ascetic emphasized total abandonment of possessions and homes, separated from what is "dead" and linked with the One who gives life. To "put on Christ" meant to leave family ties and to leave the center of the village for the margins of the wilderness.

Interestingly, the movement away from family and community was not abandonment of the familiar but a new way of being in relationship. To be a stranger in the world of late antiquity meant not to withdraw from society but to assume a special responsibility and power within it, drawn from the state of being "stranger." While Syrian ascetics withdrew from familiar surroundings, they worked zealously for congregations around them. They preached, prayed, read the Bible, and visited orphans, widows, and the sick. By imitating Christ, the holy one could do what Christ had done—intervene for divine mercy, become an instrument of divine grace in this world, and mediate between humanity and God. The ascetic was the point at which the human and holy met. Hence the Christian community turned to the ascetics in their neighborhoods—holy men and women—for cures, exorcisms, advice, as well as justice in private, public, personal, and civil affairs. Although the ascetic was seen as leaving the world, the new power of holiness found in the desert meant a new relationship with the world, and the ascetic acted as spiritual leader, carrying heavy responsibilities in relation to the larger Christian society.[14]

One of the most characteristic virtues of both Syrian and Egyptian monks was compassion. Freed from the burden of the selfish ego, the monk was reborn in the heart and attentive to the needs of the poor, the weak, and the fragile limits of the human person.

The movement into the desert of the heart forms a new relationship with the world, because one finds in the heart a depth of being that creates the world. Francis left the world of the merchant and entered the world of his heart, praying before the crucified Christ. "Because of Christ crucified," Bonaventure wrote, Francis "showed deeds of humility and humanity to lepers with a gentle piety....To poor beggars he even wished to give not only his possessions but his very self, sometimes taking off his clothes, at others altering them, at yet others, when he had nothing else at hand, ripping them in pieces to give to them."[15] Touched deeply by the compassionate love of God, Francis became the compassion of God in the world. He moved to the margins of Assisi and stayed with the lepers. There he learned to see God in a new way, in the unlovable, the ugly, and the despised. There he came to know the power of God's saving love in weak humanity. When Francis returned to the city, he carried a new awareness of God within himself and in others.

> Once when he was at Colle in the county of Perugia, Saint Francis met a poor man whom he had known before in the world. He asked him: "Brother, how are you doing?" The [man] malevolently began to heap curses on his lord, who had taken away everything he had. "Thanks to my lord, *may the Almighty Lord* curse him, I'm very bad off!"
>
> Blessed Francis felt more pity for the man's soul, rooted in mortal hatred, than for his body. He said to him: "Brother, forgive your lord for the love of God, so you may *set your*

soul free, and it may be that he will return to you what he has taken. Otherwise you will lose not only your property but also your soul." He replied, "I can't entirely forgive him unless he first gives back what he took." Blessed Francis had a mantle on his back, and said to him: "Here, I'll give you this cloak, and beg you to forgive your lord for the love of God." The man's mood sweetened, and, moved by this kindness, the man took the gift and forgave the wrongs.[16]

Instead of criticizing and judging others, Francis embraced the weak, the sick, and the disgruntled, as if each reflected the face of Jesus Christ. In the wilderness he fought the demons and in his own life he found peace by surrendering to God. He changed from being merely human to being deeply human, a change not once and for all but a new direction of being in the world. In the weakness of broken humanity, Francis experienced the compassion of God.

Meditation

Touched deeply by the compassionate love of God in the wounded flesh of Christ, Francis became the compassion of God in the world.

For Reflection

1. In the passage from *The Color Purple* how does Shug's understanding of God differ from the Christian understanding of God? How is it similar?

2. How would you explain the Incarnation—"God becoming human"—to Celie and Shug?

3. In the story from *The Assisi Compilation*, a man is changed and moved to forgiveness as a result of Francis' compassion. How would you describe the compassion of Francis in that story? What stands out the most?

4. Can you think of a time in your life when you have been changed by the compassion gesture of another person?

5. Can you think of anyone right now who might be changed by an act of compassion from you?

6. What holds you back from showing compassion in the way that Francis did in the story above?

CHAPTER THREE

The Geography of the Soul

| There is a relationship between soul and space which is being lost today, and it is this loss, I believe, which is at the heart of our ecological and economic crises. My thought is simply this: The soul needs space to grow.

Seeded in the womb of the mother, a living being grows until the space of the womb can no longer contain this unique life; it is then born into the space of the family and home. Children love the space of an open field or a shoreline and their initial response when brought into the openness of nature is to run freely, as if to chase the wind. The soul of a child expands in nature, becoming one with the soul of the earth, and for a brief moment of time human and earth share a common soul in which freedom, love, and peace abound. What then becomes of the soul as the child begins to grow in knowledge and consciousness?

In short, the geography of the soul changes; it is no longer the free open space of oneness with nature; rather, it becomes turned in upon itself, self-directed, and thus it loses the outer freedom it once enjoyed. The ills of modern culture, I believe, are rooted in the soul's loss of space or perhaps the loss of childhood.

In primal religions, the space of soul was found in the community which included both human and other living beings. To be alive, to have soul, was to share the space of being with one another in the earthly community. With evolution and the breakthrough to axial consciousness marked by autonomy, freedom, and self-transcendence, the soul became detached from the outer world of nature and anchored in the individual. It is not surprising that the redirection of soul, from nature to individual, corresponds to the rise of monotheism or belief in a personal God. The world became objectified, and the soul sought to express itself in the world by transcending the world in the womb space of a personal God.

Religion played a significant role in expanding the soul. The monk became the archetype of religious experience, as consciousness of transcendent divinity impelled the soul's choice for inner expansion and freedom. The search for identity, freedom, and self-transcendence meant a new space apart from nature. Yet as men and women sought to expand the soul's capacity for divinity by going out to the vast spaces of the desert or becoming strangers on the edge of their societies, they found a new inner space in union with divine life.

All the major religious traditions describe the need to renounce the crowded space of the family, the village or the city and to claim one's own space in the solitude of being. The Buddhist Vedic Upanishads describe how to discover the *atman*—the transcendent center of the self—through meditation. The Buddha charted the way of individual enlightenment; the Jewish prophets awakened individual moral responsibility; and Jesus went up to the mountain to pray.[1] To undergo the expansion of soul was to be freed from the confines of the ego, to become one with the divine source of life.

In the Middle Ages we find the same need for soul space, but instead of physically going out to the desert, women like the Beguines chose to go into the interior desert of the heart. They renounced the normal demands of society, marriage, and social status, and chose to live independent, prayerful lives committed to the gospel. By entering the wilderness of the heart to seek God, and identifying with the suffering God, Beguine women found an interior freedom of soul and a deep interconnectedness with humanity and the cosmos.

We see a slightly different version of this gospel life in Francis whose path was similar to the Beguines. As he lay wounded in a soldiers' hospital, Francis felt his soul dying and the need to find new space for his soul to live. Thus he left the city for the open expanse of the country, the confined space of the known into the space of the unknown. Choosing the spaciousness of the open field and the wild forest, Francis discovered the soul's capacity to expand. The outer space of the wilderness provided the inner space for the soul to grow by facing its own truth, creating its own identity and freeing the true self from the false self. The freedom of Francis' soul became for him the spaciousness of new life.

Spaciousness imbues earthly beauty. One who travels the earth knows that the beauty of different terrains—mountains and hills, peaks and valleys, urbanized cities and small country villages. The soul is like the earth, it has mountains and hills, peaks and valleys expressed in its powers of expansion, contraction, intelligence, and simplicity. Space creates soul, and the wider and more diverse our space, the more we grow as persons.

The problem of our own age is not just one of soul but one of space. The industrialization of society, the urbanization of cities, the rise of modern science, and the collapse of religion in culture, has caused the space of the soul to shrink considerably. We live in our own private worlds where the space of solitude is so small and narrow that we jealously covet it and grudgingly share it. We are so concerned not to lose the little space of soul that is our own that we often ignore it rather than dwell within it. We seek our identity and freedom not interiorly in the space of our souls but exteriorly in world and culture. We are blind to our own inner spaciousness, unaware of the capacity within us to create our own identity. The cry of our age is for "my space," the space we can call our own, create ourselves, and in which we express our personality, discover our identity, and become a human person. The crisis of our age is one of space; thus it is a crisis of soul.

Space and Identity in Francis

Space played a significant role in the life of Francis because it provided the growth of his compassionate soul. As Francis withdrew into the wilderness of the desert, he entered into the spaciousness of God's love. Alone in the desert, he was one with God.

One of the famous lines of the *Fioretti* is the prayer heard by one of the friars who saw Francis praying in a garden before the cross: "Who are you, O Lord, and who am I?" Looking at his own humanity in the mirror of the cross, Francis wondered what he saw. "Who are you, O God?"

Is this not the question of every age, every person, every seeker whether or not we name the mystery that claims our lives as God or Allah or Elohim or Mystery? Who is this God, the One who is so much more than ourselves, yet who claims us in a deep, personal way?

Francis experienced God as overflowing goodness, a superabundant love spilling over into creation and into his own personal life. The "You" of the question is the deep unquenchable source of love that

Francis experienced, a fecundity of love generating the life of the "I" which, by nature of love's overflow, belongs to the "You." Francis discovered that his "I" depends on a "Thou," and as he wondered about the direction of his life, he marveled at the source of his life. Could Francis have discovered this God of overflowing love in the city or in the shop of the merchant or in the midst of his friends? Why did he have to leave all to find God? What blocked his vision of God in the city?

The answer is space. The city can crowd the space that is needed for the soul to expand. For the Word of God to be planted in the soul, and for the soul to expand in love, space is needed. The space required for the expansion of soul is not so much physical space as it is emotional, psychological space. Place does not necessarily define space, but space determines place, as Bonaventure wrote: "You exist more truly 'where you love than where you merely live.'"[2] Where you have freedom in love, the space to be yourself, there you truly exist. A story is told of a woman who served a long time in prison. While in her small cell, she became familiar with the Bible and learned the art of prayer. She became so deeply imbued with the love of God that she was able to help other women prisoners in their struggles. Although confined to a tiny, barren prison cell, prayer had opened up for her the spaciousness of God's infinite love. When her sentence was completed, she did not want to return to the world because she had found her spacious freedom in God in the physical confines of a prison.

This story contrasts with that of a religious sister I knew who enjoyed a comfortable life in the convent with all her needs met by the community; yet this sister was always unhappy and complaining about someone or something. While she enjoyed the spaciousness of a large convent, including her own car, room, and job, her psychological and emotional space was diminished by her self-preoccupation. No matter where she went, whether on retreat, to visit her family or out to eat, she was never satisfied and always felt that the other person had gotten the better deal. Consequently, her prayer life was diminished as well.

Although we associate space and place (for example, the saying "home is where the heart is"), they are not necessarily related. Rather, inner space shapes outer place, or place—*where you love*—is a function of space—*where you truly exist*.

By this I mean if the space of our souls is shrunk to a tiny core or lost altogether, then the largest of places will not satisfy us. We could live a "super-sized life" in a super-sized house on a super-sized piece of property, but our lives will feel small, insignificant, and perhaps worthless. Having the largesse of physical place, we can feel the smallest of spiritual space and thus we may find ourselves running from activity to activity, from store to store, from dinner to dinner, friend to friend, a frenetic pace of activity that leaves us at the end of the day bone-weary and unfulfilled. By filling up our time with endless activities, we have shrunk the space within us. The shortening of time and space is the shortening of life. We may live a long life physically, but we may die early by suffocating the soul-space within us.

The Space of Personality

What is it about the spaciousness of soul that is essential to the generativity of life? The life of Francis (as with many of the saints) indicates that soul is the place of personality, and space is necessary for the ongoing creation of soul. Francis went into the space of the wilderness to enter his heart—the core of his soul—to know what he was and what he was not. Identity is a function of space and space shapes identity insofar as space provides encounter between divine and human—for example—the space of prayer.

As we come to be who we are called to be in relation to God (identity), God shows himself to the universe through his constant and continual creation of the self. The self that comes to be through a union with God is the self in which God is reflected, that is, the image of God. We come to know ourselves in God when we have the freedom to be ourselves without guile; not the self I think I need to be, as Thomas Merton wrote. Rather we seek the self God continues to create, the self that is of God and belongs to God.

Francis prayed, "Who are You, O Lord, and Who Am I?" The "I" is not a given, as Francis discovered; it is in the process of being formed in relation to a "Thou," the "You" of God. As Francis deepened his life in prayer, his understanding of himself and the world around him began to change. The grace of God turned him in a new direction, the path of knowing himself as weak and lovable; small and great; sinner and redeemed. Identity is not a given but a creative process. It is continuously emerging in the space of soul where the outer world enters the inner world and the inner world in turn creates the outer world. Identity—the truth hidden in the seed of love God has planted within—needs space to grow. The self is not a static thing; rather, it is a constellation of powers that has the potential to grow into the fullness of a single life whose reality is known to God alone. We may grow in a particular place, but it is really the space in which we have the freedom to be ourselves that influences development of our self as person. Freedom is not uncoerced space; rather it is the paradox of space where the self can accept its limits and, in doing so, open up to others.

The space of the wilderness made Francis a brother because in the freedom to be himself he recognized his need for others. He recognized himself not to be above others or apart from others but deeply related to others because he and all creation shared in the same primordial goodness that flowed from the heart of God.

Thomas Merton had a similar experience of humanity which he described in his famous awakening on the corner of Fourth and Walnut Streets in Louisville, Kentucky. In his *Conjectures of a Guilty Bystander* he writes:

> In Louisville, at the corner of Fourth and Walnut, in the center of the shopping district, I was suddenly overwhelmed with the realization that I loved all those people, that they were mine and I theirs, that we could not be alien to one another even though we were total strangers. It was like waking from a dream of separateness, of spurious self-isolation in a special world, the world of renunciation and supposed holiness. The whole illusion of a separate holy existence is a dream.
>
> . . .
>
> Then it was as if I suddenly saw the secret beauty of their hearts, the depths of their hearts where neither sin nor desire nor self-knowledge can reach, the core of their reality, the person that each one is in God's eyes. If only they could all see themselves as they really *are*. If only we could see each other that way all the time. There would be no more war, no more hatred, no more cruelty, no more greed.... I suppose the big problem would be that we would fall down and worship each other. But this cannot be *seen*, only believed and "understood" by a peculiar gift.[3]

Compassion needs space because love needs a place of unimpeded encounter between grace and nature. In a world crowded by information, we need to find space for the soul to grow.

Meditation

If the space of our souls is shrunk to a tiny core or lost altogether, then the largest of places will not satisfy us.

For Reflection

1. What do you think is the relationship between Merton's experience of solitude and space as a Trappist monk, and his experience of connectedness on the corner of Fourth and Walnut?

2. Are there places where you can go to experience solitude and space? If not, what are other ways that you can cultivate a sense of solitude and space wherever you are?

3. What are the obstacles for creating "soul" space in your life? What steps can you take to remove those obstacles?

4. Find a space where you can be yourself. Be attentive to your heart, your feelings, and your senses. Think of the people in your life; meditate on God. Write down what is most important for you at this time.

The Pillars of Poverty and Humility

| I have been talking about soul, space, and wilderness, but there is a relation of these to spiritual poverty, the type of poverty that is blessed with a community of friends in the reign of God. Francis' sense of companionship was not born of romanticism but a deep sense of brotherhood. "What allowed Francis entry into this experience of the fraternity of all creation was the asceticism of poverty."[1] Leonardo Boff explains that poverty "is a way of being by which the individual lets things be what they are; one refuses to dominate them, subjugate them, and make them the objects of the will to power."[2] Such an embrace of poverty requires "a renunciation of the instinct to power and to dominion over things."[3] Possessive power makes true communication between persons and with creation impossible. Poverty of being is letting go of the need to control and possess and recognizing our need for one another.

As Francis became poor he became open to fraternity. Poverty was the way into the experience of universal brotherhood. Through poverty Francis recognized his own creatureliness, one creature among many creatures, one poor person amid the poverty of creation. He realized that, as a creature, he was "not over things, but together with them, like brothers and sisters of the same family."[4]

The poverty of creation reflects a God of gracious and generous love. Indeed, the only reason for anything to exist, according to Bonaventure, is the free gift of God's overflowing love. The universe comes into being because God loves it and wills to give God's self to it. Michael and Ken Himes state:

> Utterly dependent, creation is divinely gifted. Thus, to see creation as a whole or any creature in particular as what it is, namely, totally dependent on the gracious will of God, is to see revealed the grace which is its foundation in being. Since everything that is exists because of the free act of God— the overflowing *agape* that is the source of all being—then everything is a sacrament of the goodness and creative power of God.[5]

The poverty of created existence reveals the richness of divine presence, and in the poverty of creation, the human person is the fullest revelation of God. Poverty means receptivity, and creation is the womb of God's grace. Bonaventure indicated that the human person is "the poor one in the desert" simply because she or he is created. Although humans originally stood upright in creation, meaning that they had their heads pointed in the right direction—toward God—they were originally poor, for they had been created out of nothing by God. As long as humans recognized and accepted their own poverty, they knew God. But when humans refused to be poor, they desired to possess rather than receive. This is the root of sin, Bonaventure claims, because humans chose to love their own good rather than receive the goods of the divine Giver.

Bonaventure goes on to say that when we accept poverty as creatures we possess all because we possess God. Once we refuse that poverty in the desire to possess things we end up with nothing. In our refusal to accept the poverty of our humanity, we may end up destroying ourselves.

Francis of Assisi had a profound understanding of poverty as it relates to the human condition. His understanding of poverty goes hand in hand with his understanding of sin. In his "Second Admonition" he spoke of sin as self-appropriation. Just as when we eat we consume or take in things for ourselves, so too sin entered into the human condition when we started consuming for ourselves, symbolized by eating from the tree forbidden by God (Genesis 2:17). Francis described sin as one of appropriating the gift of liberty and exalting ourselves over the goodness that surrounds us. To take what does not belong to us, to claim it as our own, and to use it for personal advancement is sin. Francis therefore would describe sin as: grasping, appropriating, or grabbing; self-exalting, and self-aggrandizing.

The question is, what belongs to us? Ownership may be a legal right, but possessiveness is a value, an attitude. Only when we live as poor persons do we recognize that the goods of this world do not belong to us and thus we may not possess them. Rather, they are gifts from God. To live in receptivity to the gift of God's goodness in creation is to live as a poor person, open to and dependent on the good of the human person, the good of the earth, and the good of the cosmos. When we claim the good as our own and refuse to share the goods of our lives, we miss the mark of God's justice; this is sin.

The Blindness of Sin

Sin, in Bonaventure's thought, is a turning away from God and a turning toward self in such a way that we become bent over, blinded in intellect, and entangled in an infinite number of questions. We wander about in world looking for goodness (or love) because we are unable to recognize it in our midst. Blinded in intellect and distorted in our desires, we start grabbing and clinging for ourselves what does not truly belong to us. Instead of being poor persons radically dependent on God, we make ourselves little gods and centers of our universe. We use everything for our own purposes, and we take from others what does not rightly belong to us.

When we strip the world of the common good that is God's gift to creation, we create a new system of poverty. We move from the true poverty of radical dependence to the false poverty of greed. We think we never have enough, and thus we set out to acquire more and more things at the expense of other people and the nonhuman creation itself. The sin of refusing our poverty is injustice. Our need to accumulate and possess everything can separate us from other people and the natural world, and we lord it over others through domination and power. We lose our sense of piety or true relatedness. The world becomes not only stripped of its goodness, but relationships are broken because we fail to recognize our dependence on one another, and thus we fail to acknowledge our dependence on God.

Bonaventure says that the sin of humans is really sin against the Son of God. The human desire for power is sin against the One who is the perfect image of God and thus equal to God. The Son of God, he says, accepts the poverty of the human condition to show that equality with God is not something to grasp. On the cross, God himself becomes poor. The poverty of the cross, Bonaventure indicates, is a mystery of poverty because on the cross God is not "possessing" but fully "communicating" the mystery of his love in his radical openness to and acceptance of the human person. In the crucified Christ strength becomes weakness, the powerful God becomes the poor man. Poverty is manifest in the historical career of Jesus and expressed in the naked figure on the cross who invites us to follow him, placing our absolute trust in God alone. The mystery of poverty is the recreation of the human person where one can stand before God without demands. Poverty returns one to the center of original innocence because it is fulfillment of new law which does not promise temporal goods but love.

Poverty and Relationships

We might think that Francis arrived at a deep understanding of poverty through renunciation of his material possessions. But this is not entirely true. Nowhere did he write of living *sine rebus hiuis mundi* (without the things of this world) or in destitution. Usually he wrote of living *sine proprio*, that is, without anything of one's own.

The central question of poverty, for Francis, was: What can I really call my own? Although material poverty was important to him, it was not the goal. Rather, material poverty was an outward sign of a much deeper, interior poverty. We might say that material poverty is sacramental in nature. It points to an interior poverty of spirit that Jesus proclaimed: "Blessed are the poor in spirit, for theirs is the kingdom of heaven" (Matthew 5:3).

Material poverty is the first not the final step toward true poverty in which we recognize that everything we have, including our lives, is gift. Without material poverty, true poverty is difficult to nurture. But without true poverty, material poverty is absurd. In the quest for wholeness, poverty must be sacramental in nature, a continuous striving to live more deeply in the spirit of nonpossessiveness.

Francis was a keen observer of the human condition and his understanding of poverty as the core of humanity came from the everyday lessons of life—living with others. Although Francis rarely spoke of poverty in his writings (which is surprising since others made poverty the characteristic mark of his life), he did highlight three areas in which poverty is placed in an everyday context as we seek right relationship with God: (1) our inner selves, (2) our relations with others, and (3) our relations with God.[6]

With regard to the inner self, Francis saw how human persons cling to the gifts that God has given them, for example, skills, wisdom, knowledge, ability with language, good looks, and riches while lording these over others. In one of his Admonitions he says "those people are put to death by the letter, who only wish to know the words alone, that they might be esteemed wiser than others."[7] It is not unusual to encounter those who want to "show off" their knowledge or win an argument or have the last or most intelligent word. The human person clings to knowledge as a possession that distinguishes him or her over and above others. Such a person, according to Francis, is not poor.

Similarly, the person who is preoccupied with himself or herself whether it be with regard to health, family, work, honor or reputation, is not poor. Did you ever meet someone where the entire conversation is focused on his or her job, family, or health? Where a person is so preoccupied by his or her self that it would not matter if you were an earthworm or a tadpole or whether or not you were listening? Such a person is not poor. The poor person withdraws, not out of self-pity but out of humility, creating space for another to be oneself and to enter into one's life on his or her own terms. This withdrawal is a type of "letting go," creating space so that the other person can come into being. The Jewish mystical doctrine of Tsimtsum states that the One who is omnipresent and omnipotent and who fills all things creates by withdrawing. God creates a space within God by withdrawing, so that the not-God, the other, may come into being.[8]

Although God lets go so that we may exist, we do not let go easily, and we tend to cling to things. Francis indicated that we cling to attitudes and behaviors, as much as we cling to our material possessions. I have known people who cling to past hurts with the intensity of a fresh wound even though the person who sparked their emotional outrage has long been dead. People possess the ghosts of the past with tenacity, refusing to let go and live in the present. They are not poor persons, and they usually fail to enjoy the presence of God's love.

Francis considered anger, or being disturbed at the sin of another, as the mark of possessiveness. He suggested that we should turn our attention to the sinner rather than the sin. Otherwise we cling to our anger and become upset because we self-righteously judge the one who sins.[9] Anger can turn prayer into a pancake—thin and flat—preventing us from being opened up to God because we are too filled up with ourselves.

In "Admonition Fourteen," for example, Francis writes: "There are many who, while insisting on prayers and obligations, inflict many abstinences and punishments upon their bodies. But they are immediately offended and disturbed about a single word which seems to be harmful to their bodies or about something which might be taken away from them. These people are not poor in spirit."[10] Francis' words remind us of Paul's warning to the Corinthians: "If I give away all my possessions, and if I hand over my body so that I may boast, but do not have love, I gain nothing" (1 Corinthians 13:3).

Francis, like Paul, reminds us that, without love, material poverty is worthless and perhaps sinful. What we are called to do as poor persons is to "let go and let God"—let go of everything we cling to and allow God to be the center of our lives; not to possess anything (or anyone) for ourselves but to possess God alone.

Of course, the primary center of human possession is the will. This is our most valuable center because it is the very core of our attachments. The will is the source of free choice, the decision-making center of the human person. It is most vulnerable because it can be easily threatened. We cling to our will when we are challenged or threatened in our personhood. When it comes to the will, we even like to barter with God. We say things like, "I will stop eating junk food if God makes me thin" or "I will go to church again if God makes me rich." The will in Francis' view is the place of freedom and the root of sin because here we decide if we will grab and appropriate for ourselves or share with others.

Francis perceived that the gravity of the self-centered will can be transformed only by other-centeredness. The virtue of obedience in his view can be a means of transformation because obedience requires a listening to another and letting go of our wills out of love for one another. Obedience does not require a superior, commanding officer or a demanding parent. Rather, obedience can take place between friends, lovers, family, or in community. Obedience does not mean a hierarchy of order, a top-down chain of command, but a relationship of mutuality whereby the power of love is greater than the power of self-will. Rooted in the power of love, obedience becomes an expression of poverty, letting go of what we have made our own and entrusting ourselves into the hands of another. Obedience does not demand so much to do the will of another but to listen to the other (*audire*) and to give oneself to the other out of love.

Jesus was the model of true obedience, according to Francis, because he desired nothing other than to do the will of the Father, that is, to love the Father unto death. Obedience therefore can restore our fallen self-will and direct us to the will of God. God's will is God's love for us, even as that love comes to us through our relationships with others. Without obedience we become isolated and privatized individuals, locked up and enclosed within ourselves and therefore cut off from God's love seeking to embrace us in the ordinary human person and in the ordinary goodness of nonhuman creation.

Obedience, as the fruit of poverty, manifests itself in right relationships of community. Francis saw poverty as the basis of community because poverty is the basis of interdependence. When we are in need, we are dependent on others. He saw Christ as the model and center of community because just as Jesus lived on alms and was poor, so too, our poverty means to be dependent on others [and thus on God]. In short, ownership can make community impossible because when I own things in a spirit of possession, I do not need others. Ownership as possessiveness can create self-sufficiency, independence, and therefore divisiveness. The spirit of possessiveness can place one over and against others.

What Francis indicated is that neither work nor shared vision brings people together but the Spirit of love. Poverty as radical dependence is the language of love, a concern for one another. It is the language that says "I need you, your gifts, your goodness, your ideas, and your help. Who and what you are is essential to me because without you I really cannot be me." Thus poverty speaks the language of love for one another because it says, "I need you to help complete my life." Unless we are willing to let go of what we cling to in relation to one another, we fail in poverty and thus we fail to appreciate the gifts of God's love planted in each unique human being. Poverty of heart, Johannes Metz writes, is the way we experience the warm fullness of human existence:

We must forget ourselves in order to let the other person approach us. We must be able to open up to him to let his distinctive personality unfold—even though it often frightens and repels us. We often keep the other person down, and only see what we want to see; then we never really encounter the mysterious secret of his being, only ourselves. Failing to risk the poverty of encounter, we indulge in a new form of self-assertion and pay the price for it: loneliness. Because we did not risk the poverty of openness (Matthew 10:39), our lives are not graced with the warm fullness of human existence. We are left with only a shadow of our real self.[11]

Poverty tells us of the deepest truth of our human existence; that we are created by God and are dependent on God. It is the sister of humility and helps us realize that *all* we have *is gift*. Humility (from the Latin *humus* or earth/clay) is standing with two feet on the ground; it is our earthy reality. The humble person who lives by self-knowledge, accepts one's life with its strengths and weaknesses, responding to life with the gift of being. Humility can open one to the renewing spirit of grace and make possible the return of creation to the Father. Thomas Merton said that if we were truly humble we would not bother about ourselves at all, only with God.[12]

Such an idea seems possible only for the saints. Yet when we are free from attachments, from clinging to things, then we are able to pursue our spiritual goals, to really live in love and devote ourselves to a life of adoration. This does not mean turning our attention away from earth to an imaginable place called heaven. Rather, to adore God is to see the goodness of every created thing on this marvelous planet earth. It is to realize that everything is God-filled presence, sharing in the abundance of love.

Francis spoke of humility as the sister of holy poverty. Poverty and humility allow us to contemplate the goodness of God in creation because they make us free to see things for what they are, unique, unrepeatable loved-into-being gifts of God. Only one who can taste the world and see it as an expression of God's love, is one who renounces the spirit of possessing it. On the level of human relationships poverty and humility allow us to be open to one another, to receive and share with one another. Just as the persons of the Trinity are distinguished by their sharing of love, so too, poverty and humility form true human community. Barbara Fiand says "the blessedness of the poor, it would seem (that which unites persons [in the true sense of that term]. . . and has them stand in solidarity with each other), is their *need* and, even more so, their *knowledge* of their need, for it is *this* that renders them open, receptive, grateful."[13] Only care for one another truly humanizes life. Those who are open and empty enough, who can receive and give forth what they have received, teach us that poverty is our path into God.

Poverty and humility are the pillars of compassion. When we do not possess but live in openness to and dependent on one another, we live with a capacity for compassion. We find an example of Francis' practice of poverty and compassion in his "Letter to a Minister" where he exhorts one of his brothers (most likely a guardian or leader of a certain place) to respond to a "difficult" brother with a listening heart. Francis tells the minister that love must be his priority even if a brother is obstinate or aggressive. The leader must be a listener of the Spirit, attentive to the presence of God in the brother, whose life he is to guide. The minister may at times want to flee from his responsibilities, but he must remain faithful to love the brother rather than avoid conflict. Even if the minister wants to punish or rebuke the "problem brother" he must refrain from doing so, for love conquers sin and is stronger than death. This is the way of true leadership, Francis indicates, to love those in one's care as a mother loves her son. He goes on to say:

> And if you have done this, I wish to know in this way if you love the Lord and me, His servant and yours; that there is not any brother in the world who has sinned—however much he could have sinned—who, after he has looked into your eyes, would ever depart without your mercy, if he is looking for mercy. And if he were not looking for mercy, you would ask him if he wants mercy. And if he would sin a thousand times before your eyes, love him more than me so that you may draw him to the Lord; and always be merciful with brothers such as these.[14]

Love, not sin, held priority for Francis, as it should for us. When we see only the weaknesses of another or judge another by their wrong actions, we fail to see the goodness of God within them. Francis asks us to let go of our judgments and criticisms of one another and to love with compassion. We are to act with mercy—*misericordia* which means to let the misery of others touch us in our poverty of heart.

Our tendency is to the opposite—to judge, condemn, punish, and cling to our wounds. But Francis understood that love alone heals. Compassion is the poverty of love that can reach out, even in the face of opposition, and embrace. For love heals what the human person suffers, and the one who is healed can be made whole and in turn help heal another.

Meditation

Poverty of being is letting go the need to control and possess and recognizing our need for one another.

For Reflection

1. How do you see poverty and humility related? How does your experience of obedience relate to your practice of poverty and humility?

2. Meditate on the mercy of God in your life. Write down one or two experiences of mercy that have made a difference for you. Reflect on how you have shown mercy to others.

3. Practice poverty of heart by doing the following: If someone is angry at you today or you are angry with someone, let it go; if you feel hurt, let it go; if you are too busy to have a personal conversation, stop what you are doing and enter into conversation. Take one hour for silent prayer today.

4. Reflect on the words of Johannes Metz on page 43: "Because we did not risk the poverty of openness (Matthew 10:39), our lives are not graced with the warm fullness of human existence. We are left with only a shadow of our real self."

5. What insights from this chapter are most important to you? In what areas do you need to grow?

CHAPTER FIVE

The Seeds of Compassion

| We live in an age of "globalized superficiality,"[1] bombarded by information on every level and unable to process information with any great depth. The world runs on numbers, and the human person has been swallowed up by statistics. We need a new set of values today that can unify us, something more deeply human that can link us heart to heart. Compassion is the shared experience of creaturely life. It unites what is divided and binds together what is otherwise opposed. Compassion grows out of seeds of love within the human heart. It is born from the deepest center within and unites our deepest selves.

The word *compassion* has a sense of empathy or sympathy; the word in Tibetan literally means "noble heart." Mary Jo Meadows defines compassion as "the quivering of the heart in response to another's suffering."[2] Compassion is the ability to "get inside the skin of another" in order to respond with loving concern and care. It is a deep connectedness to another; one breathes in the pain of the other and breathes out compassion. The compassionate person identifies with the suffering of others in such a way that she or he makes a space within the heart to allow the suffering of another to enter, not to heal them or remove their pain but to be with them in solidarity.

Compassion needs space within one's being because it is love reaching out and taking in. Compassion begins not with the will to love but with the recognition that one is loved. Hence, compassion begins with God. The Old Testament prophet Hosea speaks of God as tender-hearted, a God of infinite compassion. Hosea writes:

> When Israel was a child, I loved him, and out of Egypt I called my son. / The more I called them, the more they went from me; they kept sacrificing to the Baals, and offering incense to idols. / Yet it was I who taught Ephraim to walk, I took them up in my arms; but they did not know that I healed them. / I led them with cords of human kindness, with bands of love. / I was to them like those who lift infants to their cheeks. I bent down to them and fed them. / They shall return to the land of Egypt, and Assyria shall be their king, because they have refused to return to me. (11:1–5)

This God of deep compassionate love is revealed in Jesus Christ. Love poured out from the heart of Christ reflects the outpouring love of the Father for the Son in the love of the Spirit. The self-gift of the Father to the Son reflects a self-emptying already within the heart of God in such a way that we may think of the cross first in the heart of God before it is in the heart of creation. The very act of creation reflects something of a "divine crucifixion," for in creation God reveals his power to be his unconditional love for the world. The act of descending into what is nothing (creation) in order to express himself is God's humility, his condescension, his going outside his own riches to become poor.[3] God is outward-moving love, deeply in love with creation because the Father is deeply in love with the Son and yearns for the Son as a mother her child. Hans Urs von Balthasar writes: "It is God's going forth into the danger and the nothingness of the creation that reveals [God's] heart to be at its origin vulnerable; in the humility of this vulnerability lies God's condescension [humility] and thus his fundamental readiness to go to the very end of love on the cross."[4]

Bonaventure held that the cross reveals to us the heart of God because it reveals the vulnerability of God's love. The cross of Jesus Christ is the compassionate love of God which Francis experienced at San Damiano. He felt himself embraced by a God bending low in love. That is why he placed a high emphasis on the humility of God because he knew God not to be mighty or superior in power but hidden and lowly, in the crib, the cross and the Eucharist. He recognized that the power of God is divine love embracing fragile humanity and transforming death into life. Francis saw this dynamic love in a special way in the Eucharist, the Body of Christ. Through this Body he learned to embrace creation in compassion:

> Let everyone be struck with fear,
> let the whole earth tremble,
> and let the heavens exult
> when Christ, the Son of the living God,
> is present on the altar in the hands of a priest!
> O wonderful loftiness and stupendous dignity!
> O sublime humility!
> O humble sublimity!
> The Lord of the universe,
> God and the Son of God,
> so humbles Himself
> that for our salvation
> He hides Himself

under an ordinary piece of bread!
Brothers, look at the humility of God,
and pour out your hearts before Him!
Humble yourselves
that you may be exalted by Him!
Hold back nothing of yourselves for yourselves,
that He Who gives Himself totally to you
may receive you totally![5]

The great Carmelite mystic Elizabeth of the Trinity wrote to her Prioress, "Let Yourself Be Loved."[6] That is, let God be the God of your life; let go of all the things you think you need to be or of the things you think you need to do. Stop trying to control your life and your destiny and allow yourself to be loved by God who accepts you as you are, in your truest self, and desires you as you are, with all your fragile limits. This God of compassionate love is closer to you than you are to yourself. God knows your pain and your sufferings: God is the compassionate One.

When Francis entered the wilderness, he was frightened, but he began to pray and to recognize that he was not alone. In meeting God he experienced not judgment but deep compassionate love. This experience of love changed the direction of his life, and he realized that love heals what sin divides. As his ego was transformed by the embrace of God, he softened his control of other creatures, realizing the fragility and weakness of even the smallest of creatures. When we reflect on Francis' life, we see that compassion evoked the godliness of his life, expressing itself as an inner freedom to love.

Francis prayed the psalms and was particularly inspired by the psalms of suffering. He composed an "Office of the Passion" to cultivate inner freedom, empathy, and compassion. As he attracted companions around him, he recognized his dependence on the brothers to help him. He also saw that his followers would need to cultivate spiritual practices to ground them amidst the disorienting terrain of their gospel adventure. As time went on and their challenges became more numerous, they found ways to develop and adjust spiritual practices which were suited to their way of life, practices which would reflect their experience of the Christ. The "Office of the Passion" may well represent one of these practices.

The experience of the Crucified was neither at the beginning nor end of Francis' life but encompassed his entire journey. Throughout his life—probably every day in fact—Francis actively cultivated this compassion for the crucified Christ, as shown in his "Office of the Passion." He intuitively knew that his conversion could not be sustained simply on the emotional energy of his initial religious experience.

To use a contemporary analogy, a person in recovery from alcoholism may find the Serenity Prayer helpful at first. But if recovery is to be maintained, the prayer needs to be deepened, interiorized, and expanded upon.

The "Office of the Passion" was one way in which Francis expanded upon his initial encounter with the Crucified Christ and kept the insight of that encounter alive throughout his life. The high level of textual variation in the manuscript tradition surrounding "Office of the Passion" tells us that it probably evolved over a long period of Francis' life.[7] It was a working document—always a work in progress—because it was a lived prayer.

The genre of the "Office of the Passion" was not original to Francis. The practice of constructing prayers from personally selected verses of Psalms in a freestyle manner was not uncommon in the Middle

Ages. But how Francis chose to put these psalms together—and his method of editing, adding, and subtracting lines of the psalms—tells us a great deal about how he interpreted the meaning and significance of the Passion in his own life. The anthropologist René Girard sees the Passion as the culmination of Old Testament hopes and promises, especially as described in Psalms, which the early Christians looked to for guidance. He writes:

> In studying the Passion we are struck by the role played by quotations from the Old Testament, particularly from the Psalms. The early Christians took these references seriously, and the so-called allegorical or figurative interpretation in the Middle Ages involved the expansion and appropriate amplification of this New Testament practice. Modern critics generally, and mistakenly, have no interest in this. They tend more to a rhetorical and strategic interpretation of the quotations.[8]

Francis of Assisi was one of those medieval individuals who expanded and amplified the New Testament practice of using passages from the Old Testament to understand or shed light on the New Testament. When one prays or reads the psalms of the "Office of the Passion," at least two significant elements emerge: first, they are in the voice of the victim; and second, they cultivate empathy in the reader. Girard writes:

> Particularly in the penitential Psalms, we see the word shift from the persecutors to the victims, from those who are making history to those who are subjected to it. The victims not only raise their voices but are also vociferous even in the midst of their persecution. Their enemies surround

them and prepare to strike them. Sometimes the latter retain the monstrous, animal appearance they had in mythology; these are the packs of dogs or herds of bulls, "strong beasts of Bashaan." Yet these texts are torn from mythology, as Raymond Schwager has clearly shown: they increasingly reject sacred ambivalence in order to restore the victim to his humanity and reveal the arbitrary nature of the violence that strikes him.[9]

The following lines, composed by Francis, could have been spoken from the mouth of a leper being who was cast out from Assisi, as from the mouth of Jesus about to be crucified:

My friends and my neighbors have drawn near
and stood against me;
those who were close to me have stayed far away.
You have driven my acquaintances far from me;
they have made me an abomination to them.[10]

The lepers lived down below in the valley, outside the gates of Assisi, and hence far from the normal flow of culture and society. They were not allowed to enter the city, and when they did so, they had to ring a bell to alert the citizens that an "untouchable" was approaching. They were relegated to the status of the "living dead" because once they were identified as leprous, they stood in a grave while their own funeral ritual was performed before their very eyes. Hence the following lines could have been uttered by a leper:

I am numbered among those who go down to the pit.
* I have become as someone without help, cut off among the*
dead.[11]

53

This same theme appears in Psalm IV:

> *Seeing me everyone laughed at me;*
> *they whispered and shook their heads.*
> *I am a worm and no human,*
> *the scorn of men and the outcast of the people.*
> *I have been made despicable to my neighbors;*
> *far beyond all my enemies,*
> *a thing of fear to all my acquaintances.*[12]

In contrast to the modern fascination with the physical violence of the Passion of Christ, such as with Mel Gibson's film *The Passion of the Christ*, these psalms focus on the interior disposition of Jesus as he suffers the fate of the victim who is cast out from society and sentenced to death. The focus is on the heart of the one who suffers. "My heart has become like melting wax in the midst of my bosom."[12]

One gets the sense that these prayers are not intended to inspire a sense of guilt in the person who prays them, but a genuine sense of empathy for the victim. Praying these prayers on a daily basis, approximately every three hours corresponding to the hours of Christ's Passion, must have had a profound effect on Francis' vision of the world. It must have raised questions on how to respond to the lament and rejection within the psalms, as it was played out in real life before Francis' eyes. Often we do not notice the persecuted victim—the scapegoat; we remove the scapegoat from our ordinary field of vision and create blind spots which make it more difficult to see the victimized innocent one. In order to notice the innocent victim, one must be willing to sift through a fog of illusion created by the dominant culture. One cannot simply search "scapegoat" on Google—one must physically try to recognize the victim as person. Girard writes:

Almost no one is aware of his [or her] own shortcoming. We must question ourselves if we are to understand the enormity of this mystery. Each person must ask what his [or her] relationship is to the scapegoat. I am not aware of my own, and I am persuaded that the same holds true for my readers. We only have legitimated enmities. And yet the entire universe swarms with scapegoats. The illusion of persecution is as rampant as ever, less tragically but more cunningly than under Guillaume de Machaut.[14]

Francis was one who reflected on the question (though he would not have used this terminology): "What is my relationship to the victim?" The manner in which he regularly prayed the "Office of the Passion" helped him to raise this question and facilitated an awareness of the innocent victims in his midst.

The "Office of the Passion" was Francis' way of developing a consciousness of compassion. He showed compassion to persons because he believed their humanity reflected God. His compassion was not "doing for" but "being with," a solidarity in love that accepted weakness as an invitation to love. The "Office of the Passion" was Francis' way of developing a consciousness of compassion. He showed compassion to persons because he believed their humanity reflected God. His compassion was not "doing for" but "being with," a solidarity in love that accepted weakness as an invitation to love. The depth of his love was one with God's compassionate love, longing for wholeness and healing, for unity and fullness of life; a love that sought to empower others. The author of *The Assisi Compilation* describes Francis walking alone one day along the road not far from the church where he heard a voice speaking to him from the cross; he was crying loudly and wailing as he went. A passerby asked him, "Brother, what's wrong?" thinking that Francis was suffering from a painful illness. But Francis was not crying out of pain or self-pity; rather he wept out of deep compassion for the crucified Christ—the abandoned God in suffering humanity. [15]

One time an older brother was greatly afflicted by a "tribulation of the flesh" and seemed to be "swallowed into the depth of despair." He was so ashamed of his thoughts that he was afraid to talk about them or confess them to anyone. One day as he was walking with Francis, the saint said to him: "Brother, from now on you do not have to confess your tribulation to anyone. *Do not be afraid.*"[16] Francis exhorted the brother to pray when he felt tempted and not to worry. He sought to restore individuals to wholeness of heart, so that they might be at peace with themselves and with others. All along he was praying the "Office of the Passion." Francis realized that a suffering brother is a suffering community, and that a brother restored to health in mind and body was a community alive in God. Such compassion was contrary to his age, however, as it is to ours. We do better at causing others to fall, or worse, we push them over the edge. Thomas of Celano wrote:

> Woe to the pitiful madness of our age!
> Not only do we not lift up or even hold the tottering,
> But often enough we push them to fall![17]

Francis sought to build up the human person in the midst of human weaknesses, to restore one's dignity as human and to show how valuable each person is in the family of creation. His way of life was hard, but his mercy was wide. The hungry needed to eat, the sick needed care, and the simple-minded required gentle guidance. He got annoyed with the brothers but greater did he love them. Once when a sick brother had a craving to eat grapes, Francis took him into the vineyard and gathered grapes from the vine and began to eat them so that the brother would not feel alone.

When a very simple man by the name of John desired to join Francis, Francis made him his special companion "because of his gift of simplicity."[18] John copied whatever gestures of movements Francis made. "If Francis spat, John would spit too; if he coughed, John would cough as well. If the saint lifted up his hands to heaven, John would raise his too, and he watched him intently as a model, turning himself into a copy of all his actions."[19] To the person who annoys us, our tendency is to ignore or rebuke them, but Francis saw in John the gift of simplicity and, although he did not like being copied, he delighted in John's simplicity. Thus he "gently told him not to do this anymore."[20]

One time the brothers' friary was invaded by robbers who stole the little food the friars had. Francis had returned to the friary after gathering food and wine for the community and heard of the incident from Brother Angelo. Whereas Angelo was angry with the robbers and wanted revenge, Francis judged that the robbers must have been hungry, so he gave the bread and wine he had collected to Angelo and ordered him to go find the robbers and to give them the extra food. Angelo could not understand this decision but went as told. He found the robbers and gave them the food as commanded by St. Francis. When the robbers heard this, they knew of their wrongdoing and repented.[21]

The genius of Francis is that he saw basic human need as motive for action. The human need of the robbers became the occasion for preaching the gospel by following the example of Jesus who ate and drank with sinners. The bread and wine that Francis begged for and that he gave to the robbers had God as its source. Francis became an instrument of God in sharing this goodness with the robbers in their need. He did not place himself above the robbers as Angelo did but was with them in their need. Francis understood that God takes on not just our humanity but our frailty. Michael Blastic writes: "When Brother Angelo saw the three robbers, he saw sin, something that disqualified their need. When Francis saw the three robbers, he saw three men who had a need, and it would not be pushing the analogy too far to say that when Francis saw the three robbers he saw Jesus Christ who took on our frailty and poverty." [22] Incarnation is salvific because it is the embrace of the human condition before any reference to sin. The compassionate person offers salvation by offering healing love.

Compassion is a way of being in relationship with another that accepts the other in his or her weakness and responds to the needs of the person with mercy. In this way, compassion is Eucharistic; it is reconciling, a continuation of the Incarnation, showing God's desire to be with us. Authentic human need invites compassion into its home. Too often we reject people in their weaknesses; we refuse those with needs different from our own needs; we have no time for the poor or weak person. We are embarrassed by the weak and we seek to avoid them because we cannot accept or believe that this weak person is God and God is here in this weak flesh. Yet without this belief we are not Christian, for this is the meaning of Eucharist, as Graziano Marcheschi captures in his poem, *Tabernacles*:

It happened fast.
A feeble-brained innocent,
  refugee from half-way spaces, moving at the wrong time:
  the Bread raised high,
  the Cup engaged in mystery,

and he chooses this time to change his seat
from one church side to the other.
For a moment his head blocks the view
Of bread yielding to miracle.
For a moment his face and the bread are one.
The words spoken over both.
Then hands shake, extending proper peace;
cheeks meet,
words wish a peace the world has never tasted.
He stares, like a dog offered too many bones at once,
and accepts only one hand's greeting.
Next comes procession to his first meal of the day
as faces clearly wonder if he understands what this is all about.
He takes the proffered piece of pita
   in this most post-Vatican assembly
and stops.
Momentarily thrown by this bread with pockets,
he's oh-so-gently reassured that it's quite all right to eat.
He takes
and green teeth masticate the Body of Christ.
Then he reaches for the syrupped goodness of the cup
(*Just three sips after him I debate the wisdom of changing lines.*)
His puffed-cheek mouthful nearly drains the cup.
(*I almost wish he had so I wouldn't need to tell myself I won't catch
some disease.*)
And then
(I *knew it!*)
he coughs
and sends forth a rosy mist

that sprays Divinity onto the floor.

A rainbow comes and goes in that unexpected spray

as gasps are quelled in forty throats.

He clamps his mouth with leaky hands

looking like child

trying to keep a pricked balloon from bursting.

Unslackened, the line moves on

and Divinity is trampled by shod feet

till pure white linen,

   —bleached and starched—

in fervent hands that won't permit impiety,

drinks the pink God from the floor.

In a corner he sits alone

in rapt humiliation.

When someone asks, "Are you O.K.?"

he quickly shows his palms and says,

"I didn't wipe them on my dirty pants, I didn't.

I rubbed them hard together, see?"

and he demonstrates, with insect frenzy, how he used friction

to evaporate the spilled God from his hands.

Oh, what a cunning God who tests our faith

by hiding in green-teethed

tabernacles

to see how truly we believe

in the miracle of real presence.[23]

Where do we draw the lines of compassion? When does the human person become excluded from our world or worthy of our rejection? When do we lose sight of our own feeble and weak humanity? Or we might ask, when do we slip into the mode of playing God?

Our greatest challenge is accepting the human person, as we encounter the human face. When we are repulsed by the poor and the weak, the stranger and the immigrant, we are repulsed by God. "It is much easier to find God in the miraculous than in the ordinary," Dawn Nothwehr writes.[24] She continues: "The green-teethed 'feeble-brained innocent' always jars me back into the reality that *the same Christ Incarnate* redeems *all people*."[25] Can we not admit that the Incarnation is difficult to believe because we cannot accept God's presence in weak, fragile humanity?

An incarnational bias is evident today in our globalized culture. The "problem" of immigrants, welfare recipients, incarcerated, mentally ill, mentally disabled, and all who are marginalized by mainstream society, is a problem of the incarnation. When we reject our relatedness to the poor, the weak, the simple, and the unlovable we define the family of creation over and against God. In place of God we decide who is worthy of our attention and who can be rejected. Because of our deep fears, we spend time, attention, and money on preserving our boundaries of privacy and increasing our knowledge and power. We hermetically seal ourselves off from the undesired "other," the stranger, and in doing so, we seal ourselves off from God. By rejecting God in the neighbor, we reject the love that can heal us.

Until we come to accept created reality with all its limits and pains as the living presence of God, Christianity has nothing to offer to the world. It is sound bites of empty promises. When we lose the priority of God's love in weak, fragile humanity, we lose the Christ, the foundation on which we stand as Christians.

Compassion *continues* the Incarnation by allowing the Word of God to take root within us, to be enfleshed in us. The Incarnation is not finished; it is not yet complete for it is to be completed in us.

It takes all that we have and all that we are to be Christian; we must throw ourselves into the arms of God's infinite love. We are called to continue the Incarnation toward the new creation, the fullness of Christ, that is, humanity and earthly being bound together in a union of love.

Let me close with a story recounted by a young Franciscan friar who experienced compassion from a Poor Clare sister in an unforgettable way. One day during his retreat, Friar Bob confided with Sr. Ellen that he was having a very hard time. He recently experienced a great loss in his life and was feeling quite sad. He could not seem to enter into prayer or enjoy the retreat very much, since he was preoccupied with his experience. As he told his story to Sr. Ellen, he broke down in tears. She gave him a small packet of tissues which she carried in her pocket. Sr. Ellen listened to him and offered him words of comfort and counsel on a bench outside the chapel. Then they went into the chapel to pray Vespers along with the rest of the group. One of the Psalms from Evening Prayer was Psalm 22. After Vespers ended, both Friar Bob and Sr. Ellen stayed behind awhile praying in silence. Then Ellen left her seat, approached Bob and sat next to him with her breviary. She put her arm around him and began to pray again out loud:

> I am wearied with all my crying
> My soul is parched
> My eyes are wasted away
> From looking for my God.

She continued with a series of other passages from Scripture which had an uncanny resonance with Bob's own experience. He later recounted this event and said that it was the most profound experience of compassion that he had ever had.

Meditation

Compassion begins not with the will to love but with the recognition that one is loved. It is not an act but an attitude, a way of being in relationship, accepting the other in his or her weakness and responding to the needs of the other with mercy.

For Reflection

1. How do you show compassion to others when they are suffering?

2. Reflect on a time when you failed to show compassion. What prevented you from reaching out? How does the "Office of the Passion" show Francis' association of compassion with God's humility, a humble God bending low in love?

3. What ways of compassion are found in Francis that may be a guide for us today?

4. In the story of the friary invaded by robbers, what character or characters can you relate to and why? What authentic human needs invite a response of compassion?

Contemplation and Compassion

| Science tells us that the development of life toward greater complexity is a growth in consciousness. Consciousness is the mental awareness of what is physically present but also an awareness that includes feelings, emotions, intuitions, as well as knowledge. The conscious person lives with attentiveness to one's experience in the world, intelligently reflective of that experience. Teilhard de Chardin said that the whole evolutionary process, from the Big Bang onward, is an unfolding of consciousness. Evolution proceeds toward greater consciousness which is active at all levels of reality; the mental enters the material world in a natural way. We used to approach problems by saying "mind over matter." Now we must grapple with the reality that mind is in matter and at the heart of matter. The development of life is a development of consciousness.

Compassion is a growth in consciousness. It is a way of being for others that flows from a mindful connectedness and our awareness of unity. Prayer deepens consciousness and in turn compassion. Prayer is that deep dialogue with the source of all Being, an opening up to new depths of relatedness and hence, new Being. It is engagement of the human person in understanding, insight, and conversion. Prayer is a dynamic movement of the spirit, an expansion of being expressed in personal and communal growth. It is an evolution of consciousness and thus a movement toward greater unity which realizes the deep interconnectivity between peoples, the earth, and all forms of life. It is that openness to grace which holds one in the silence of love's fountain fullness; the grace which frees one to express oneself truthfully, to proclaim liberty to captives and sight to the blind. Prayer is the gift of love and the invitation to die a thousand deaths so that the fullness of life may be released in the universe. Prayer is that deep "knowing-with" God—a consciousness of God to become ourselves by opening us up to freedom-in-love and, in so doing, to become the Christ. It is a movement into the Fountain—a fullness of love through the Holy Spirit, the One who makes all things new, in union with the Christ who is Alpha and Omega.

Prayer is deep dialogue with the One who is the source of our lives and in whom truth bears its fruit in freedom. When we can honestly open our hearts to God, we liberate our souls from darkness to become persons of light. We let go of what is yet incomplete, and we surrender what is unforgiven so the unlived within us may be set free. The poet John O'Donohue writes:

> May all that is unforgiven in you
> Be released.
>
> May your fears yield
> Their deepest tranquilities.
>
> May all that is unlived in you
> Blossom into a future
> Graced with love.[1]

Authentic prayer gives birth to authentic personhood because when we know ourselves in God we know ourselves as God created us— without pretense. The God-centered person lives without guile or the need to control. The divine light within becomes the guiding light of vision in the world. When we do not know ourselves or accept weakness in ourselves, we tend to judge others harshly; we become critical and biased. We see the faults in others, but we do not name them within ourselves. Francis saw himself as a great sinner and would often perform public penance to confess his weak humanity before others.

One time he tied meat around his neck and let himself be dragged into the public square to show others his weakness with regard to fasting. Another time he rolled naked in the snow after building three snowmen and addressing them as his family, showing his struggle with celibacy for the sake of the kingdom.

Francis struggled with his own human limits and thus he accepted others with their limits as well. He took to heart Jesus' words: "[F]irst take the log out of your own eye, and then you will see clearly to take the speck out of your neighbor's eye" (Matthew 7:5). It is easier to see the faults of another; it is more difficult to see those same faults in oneself. Yet, the key to compassion is conversion of self; prayer enkindles the grace of conversion. As Francis prayed, he became more deeply attuned to the experience of God in his own life which in turn deepened his compassion for others. Through prayer Francis reached the deepest oneness with God; he realized this oneness by sharing in the human poverty and humility of Christ. Compassion transformed Francis into another Christ "because of the *excess of his love.*"[2]

Compassion and Clare of Assisi

In her letters to Agnes of Prague, Clare of Assisi develops a path of prayer that leads to contemplation and compassion, and she draws these together as one spiritual process of transformation in Christ. She exhorts Agnes to gaze upon the Mirror of the Crucified Spouse each day, to spend time with the one who loves her deeply. She asks Agnes to see herself in this mirror, to "study her face," lest she go off and forget what she looks like. The author of the Letter of James writes: "[F]or they look at themselves and, on going away, immediately forget what they were like. But those who look into the perfect law, the law of liberty, and persevere, being not hearers who forget but doers who act—they will be blessed in their doing" (James 1:24–25).

Prayer that leads to contemplation leads to a penetrating vision that gets to the truth of reality. It is being drawn into the mystery of divine love incarnate in weak humanity; to feel this love, taste it, experience it in one's being, and be transformed by it. What makes us most like Christ, the image of God, Clare indicates, is one's own frail and fragile humanity. If we truly loved our own frail and fragile humanity, we would love the fragile humanity of others as well. Because we reject our own weakness, however, we reject the weaknesses of others. To penetrate the truth of reality we must first penetrate the truth of our own reality which is fragile and weak.

Clare asks Agnes to embrace her own humanness, her identity, her own experience, as that which makes her most like Christ. The mirror of the cross, which is the cross of the Crucified, reflects back to us our own humanity, as we gaze upon it. It shows us how we are like or unlike God. It reflects to us the wounds, suffering, and violence inflicted on an innocent person, such as the self-offering of Jesus' life to the Father out of love. What do we see in this mirror?

Clare says that we are to contemplate this image of the Crucified so that we "can feel what his friends feel" and taste the spirit of compassion. When we enter into the image of the Crucified Christ as the image in which we are created, we contemplate the truth of the human condition. This truth is the foundation of conversion, from selfish love to selfless love, from prayer to contemplation, by which we are transformed in love.

Richard Rohr speaks of the two gazes of prayer. "The first gaze," he says, "is seldom compassionate. It is too busy weighing and feeling itself: 'How will this affect me?' or 'How does my self-image demand that I react to this?' or 'How can I get back in control of this situation?'" Rohr states:

> This leads us to an implosion, a self pre-occupation that cannot enter into communion with the other or the moment. In other words, we first feel *our* feelings before we can relate to the situation and emotion of the *other*. Only after God has taught us how to live 'undefended' can we immediately stand with and for the other, and for the moment....
>
> [Contemplation] is not the avoiding of the distractions ...it is a daily merging with the "problem" and finding its full resolution. What you quickly and humbly learn in contemplation is that *how you do anything is probably how you do everything.* If you are brutal in your inner reaction to your own littleness and sinfulness, your social relationships and even your politics will probably be the same—brutal.[3]

In *Story of a Soul* St. Thérèse of Lisieux daily deals with her irritations, judgments, and desire to run from her fellow sisters in the convent. She faces her own mixed motives and pettiness, but her goal is always compassion and communion. She suffers her powerlessness until she can finally break through to love and, in doing so, she breaks through to the second gaze, the deep penetrating gaze that sees the truth of reality and the truth of the sisters she is living with. As Rohr states, *"She holds the tension within herself (the essence of contemplation) until she herself is the positive resolution of that tension."*[4] By committing herself to love she is resolved to let love triumph over her natural inclination for criticism or judgment; she lets the gaze of love dominate her inmost heart. By doing so, love wins. She lets go of her need to control the situation, and she surrenders herself to the moment of truth, the human face with whom she is confronted. In that face she sees the suffering face of Christ; she sees the footprint of God.

The way to compassion is first interior. Prayer must lead to the truth of one's self—our poverty, humility, and suffering. When we can identify this "footprint" within ourselves, then we can identify this "footprint" in others. The prophet cries out in the book of Lamentations, "Look and see if there is any sorrow like my sorrow" (1:12). "Look and see." What do we see when we see the face of another? Do we see ourselves in the face of another human person? Do we see the suffering face of Christ? Or do we reject what we see because it does not fit into our private worlds? At what point do we become incapable of feeling the pain of another?

Clare asks that we enter into the experience of Christ's suffering, to taste and see the love of God poured into the vessel of weak humanity. It is the prayerful experience of suffering that leads to compassion. "The mystery of God's love," the authors of *Compassion: A Reflection on a Christian Life* write, "is not that our pain is taken away, but that God first wants to share that pain with us."[5] The one who acts compassionately participates in the suffering of the other, takes another person's suffering on himself, entering into community with them and bearing their burdens.

Compassion is another name for Christian living. It is accepting the limits of our humanity without asking why. It is letting others be without projecting onto them our demands and expectations. Hence, it is believing in the human person as the hidden presence of God. To see the pain and weakness of another is to see the crucified Christ, the love of God on the face of frail humanity. It is to recognize that *this* person at *this* time is the face of Christ; *this* person is God's love incarnate. If I reject *this* person, I reject God. If I hate *this* person, I hate God. There is nothing I do to the neighbor that I do not do to God. Love of God cannot be separated from love of neighbor, for the neighbor is the very presence of God. When we reject the neighbor, we reject God. We crucify Christ over and over, adding more violence to a violent world. Thus we are to love deeply. The more deeply we love the one who suffers, the more deeply we love God.

Compassion is a heart-to-heart encounter because compassion flows from the human heart; it is not a rational conclusion to a problem. Rather, it is an act of love beyond what the mind can comprehend. The heart therefore must be able to see what may be blind to the physical eye.

Contemplation is vision of the heart; it is a penetrating gaze that gets to the truth of reality. It can be easy to miss the suffering person in our midst, our brother or sister, spouse, parent, or friend. We become so used to seeing them in a certain way that we usually project onto them what we expect to see, unaware of our blindness. In the mid-1960s there was a popular song by Smokey Robinson entitled, "The Tracks of My Tears." The song's refrain spoke poignantly of human pain hidden deep within the human heart, and how a smile on the face deceives others and masks the truth of one's sorrows. A deceptive smile can hide an abyss of tears unless one looks closely to see the "tracks of tears."

Antoine de Saint-Exupéry said that only the heart can see rightly the truth invisible to the naked eye. But the heart needs spaciousness of soul to see. Poverty creates spaciousness of the heart; living *sine proprio* creates room for others to be part of one's life and, in turn, enables one's life to be dependent on others. Modern culture tries to fill up the space of our lives with things; empty space tends to create fear. "Being busy" has become a status symbol by which we fill up every corner and time. "We are so afraid of open spaces and empty spaces," Henri Nouwen said, "we occupy them with our minds even before we are there."[6]

Open-ended questions must be resolved and situations completed. The need to fill the empty spaces of life reveals our intolerance of people and events and makes us look for labels or classification to fill the emptiness. These preoccupations prevent our having new experiences and keep us hanging on to the familiar ways. We prefer a bad certainty to a good uncertainty. How can we expect something really new to happen to us if our hearts and minds are so full of our own concerns that we do not listen to the sounds announcing a new reality? As Nouwen states: "We cannot change the world by a new plan, project or idea. We cannot change other people by our convictions, stories, advice and proposals, but we can offer a space where people are encouraged to disarm themselves, to lay aside their occupations and preoccupations and to listen with attention and care to the voices speaking in their own center."[7]

To convert hostility into hospitality and fear into friendship, we need space where we can reach out to our fellow human beings and invite them into a new relationship. This space of compassion comes when we can let go of the things that fill our minds and hearts and accept others in their weaknesses, loving them as a mother loves her child. Nouwen cautions against the "temptation of activism," getting caught up trying to solve other people's problems, which is what many of us try to do. We are called not to fix things but to bind up wounds through the power of love, realizing that the human person is strengthened when love triumphs over fear.

A Yiddish tale tells of an old wise woman who was asked, "What is the greatest burden in life? Is it helping the sick, feeding the poor or putting up with your neighbor?" She responded by saying, "It is none of these. The greatest burden of life is to have nothing to carry." Sometimes the very struggles we try to avoid are the very blessings of our lives. Each day we are invited into love, to deepen our loves, and to renew ourselves in love. Our relation to God must be in existence for others. If we give up on love, it is by our own choice. St. Paul wrote, "Love is patient; love is kind; love is not envious or boastful or arrogant or rude. It does not insist on its own way; it is not irritable or resentful; it does not rejoice in wrongdoing, but rejoices in the truth. It bears all things, believes all things, hopes all things, endures all things" (1 Corinthians 13:4-7). Compassion is unfailing love.

Meditation

What makes us most like Christ is our frail and fragile humanity. If we truly loved our own frail and fragile humanity, we would love the frailty of others as well.

For Reflection

1. Read St. Mark's Passion slowly and meditatively. Imagine you are a bystander in the crowd, observing the events. What stirs inside of you as you observe this event from a place in the crowd?

2. Now, pray the following psalm written by St. Francis (next page) for meditation on the Passion. As you pray, imagine that you are in Jesus' position, praying from the cross.

3. Then, imagine you are a leper in medieval Europe, cast out from the city to live in isolation from the rest of society. Pray this prayer as if you were that leper.

4. Then, call to mind a contemporary person you know—or someone you have heard about—who is suffering deeply, and pray the prayer with that person in mind.

5. If you are doing this as a group, discuss your reflections on this exercise. If you are doing it alone, write your reflections. What image of God emerges in this Psalm, particularly in the last third of the Psalm?

"Psalm VI"
(recalling the moment of Christ's death on the cross)

O all you who pass along the way
  look and see if there is any sorrow like my sorrow.
For many dogs have surrounded me,
  a pack of evildoers closed in on me.
They looked and stared at me;
  they divided my garments among them
  and they cast lots for my tunic.
They pierced my hands and feet,
  they counted all my bones.
They opened their mouth against me,
  like a raging and roaring lion.
I have been poured out like water
  and all my bones have been scattered.

My heart has become like melting wax
  in the midst of my bosom.
My strength has been dried up like baked clay,
  and my tongue cleaves to my jaws.
They gave me gall as my food
  and, in my thirst, vinegar to drink.
They led me into the dust of death
  and added sorrow to my wounds.
I have slept and risen
  and my most holy Father *has received me with glory.*
Holy Father, you held my right hand
  led me with your counsel
  and have taken me up with glory.
For what is there in heaven for me
  and what do I want on earth besides you?
See, *that I am God,* says the Lord
I shall be exalted among the nations
  and exalted on the earth.
Blessed be the Lord, the God of Israel
  Who has redeemed the souls of His servants
    with his very own most holy Blood
and Who will not abandon all who hope in Him.
And we know that *He is coming,*
  that He will come to judge justice.[8]

CHAPTER SEVEN

The Canticle of Compassion

| In his book *At Home in the Cosmos*, David Toolan described Francis of Assisi as a biophiliac, a lover of the earth. His love for creation flowed from being in creation, in solidarity with all creatures. Although Pope John Paul II called Francis the patron saint of ecology, the saint's path to oneness with creation was more profound than a mere love of creatures.

The root of Francis' ecological relatedness began with his encounter with God in the crucified body of Christ. Up to his conversion, Francis was an individual caught up in himself, lured by fame, fortune, and friends. By accepting the embrace of God's humble love in his own weak humanity, Francis changed from a self-isolated "I" to a relational "I–Thou." This change marked a new level of consciousness and growth into the heart of creation.

We suffer today from ecological crises on different levels. We have an energy crisis due to overconsumption of fossil fuels, a crisis of global warming because of the excess carbon in the atmosphere, an industrialization of food that disrupts food cycles and creates artificial food substances. We have depletion of natural resources, species extinction, alteration of natural life cycles, and loss of biodiversity.

In North America our ecological footprint outstrips the carrying capacity of the earth, and if we continue at our present rate of food and energy consumption, we will not have a sustainable future. We are heading into a future of ecological catastrophe, and we will not be able to meet the needs of future generations. We continue to consume the earth's resources at excessive amounts, unconscious of the consequences of our overconsumption. Invoking St. Francis as the patron saint of ecology will serve no real good unless we explore how he changed his relatedness to creation, from consumption to compassion.

The key to Francis' "ecological life" is relationship. Francis found himself to be an "I" in need of a "Thou" and realized that he could not be fully a person apart from being a brother. His relationship with God, rooted in a profound love of God and his acceptance of God's love in his own life, changed the way he knew himself in relation to others. He took the commandment of Jesus to heart, "love your neighbor as yourself" (Mark 12:31) and realized that to love oneself, one must know oneself. He prayed for knowledge before the San Damiano cross: "Give me the right feeling and knowledge so that I can carry out Your holy and true command," showing that true knowledge of oneself is found in God, and true knowledge of God is found in oneself. This knowledge of self and God is the ground on which is built the temple of love which is the home of compassion.

Love changes the way we know things. Love is not blind affection or mere satisfaction. Rather, love is the highest good that seeks and desires the highest good in another. To love is to know the good in another without questioning the good of the other or trying to understand the good of the other. The wise person is one whose knowledge is shaped by love and who sees the world through the eyes of love.

Such a person lives from a deeper center within. Rooted in the heart, the wise person is rooted in the world and sees the world in its truth and beauty. One sees from the center of the beloved; thus one sees the world unafraid of the vision. The wise person is one who has the freedom to remain empty in the face of encounter and to allow the experience of encountering the new, whether a new person, creature or idea, to enter one's life and change one's capacity to love.

In the movie *Billy Elliott* there is a poignant scene where the father confronts his son, Billy, in the neighborhood auditorium. The father is enraged by his son's passion for ballet while he is struggling without work and money. The father's fury is written on his stone face, as he glares at the son showing his friend the steps of ballet. The son is at first petrified by the father's fury and then he begins to dance. As he dances, Billy is freed from his fear and leaps into the air, dancing pirouettes with a lightness of freedom. The father realizes the harm he has done by depriving his son of the gift of ballet. Moved by compassion for his son, the father returns home determined to help his son realize his dream.

Love creates space for compassion because love secures one in something greater than oneself, enabling a person to go beyond oneself for another. When we know by way of love or wisdom, we can touch, taste, and experience the other as good and not threatening or dangerous. It is a subject-to-subject relatedness, a oneness of being that transcends the differences of opposition. I am drawn by the face of another not because the other's face is different from mine (although I can be drawn by the stranger who makes up in me what I lack in myself), but because we share the same humanity and thus we are sister and brother.

Compassion deepens when we see each other eye to eye. Not too long ago, someone told me the story of a homeless woman who was attacked by a man intending to rape her. She grabbed his wrist and looked him in the eye and said, "Sir, there is nothing you can do to harm me, but if you rape me you will destroy your own manhood because you will reduce yourself to something less than human." He looked at her and stopped, realizing his wrongdoing.

Through courage and compassion, violence can be transformed. Francis used to say "the love of him who loved us is greatly to be loved"; he was inspired by all creation to the love of God.[1] His life shows us that love has the power to change hearts and in turn to change the world.

The Experience of Knowledge

Francis lived in a premodern age and thus he was not confronted by the complexities of science and modern culture. One of the main problems today with regard to living compassionately is the way we know the world.

Before the Middle Ages, monastic theology was the primary means of knowledge, based on prayerful reading of the Scriptures, the experience of God, and reflection on that experience. Although Francis was not trained in Latin, he possessed a type of experiential knowledge. He was not an abstract thinker nor did he take abstract knowledge from things; his was not "objective" knowledge. Rather, Francis' way of knowledge involved the body as much as the mind. It was different from scholastic theology which proceeded by deductive arguments to arrive at an unbiased or objective conclusion. Francis knew by way of experience. Through his senses of touch, taste, smell, hearing, and vision, he took in the world of creatures as he encountered them and returned to the world of creatures their own dignity and being. He let things be themselves and in being themselves Francis saw the beauty of God.

When modern philosophy arose along with modern science, the question of true knowledge became problematic. René Descartes, Jesuit-trained and zealously Catholic, sought to find pure truth and certainty apart from the changing world of created reality. He found this certainty within himself. The only truth, he said, was in himself as a thinking subject, all else was a mere extension of matter. His philosophy was highly influential on the development of Western thought, giving rise to separation of mind and spirit, body and soul, an unhealthy dualism that has supported the individualism of our own age. By separating true knowledge from experience of the world, Descartes stripped the world of its sacred character. The material world became lifeless and inert, a world of things to be manipulated. Thanks to Descartes and others, such as Francis Bacon, the world of creation lost its subjectivity and became an object of human control and experimentation.

Today our process of knowledge begins with the self-thinking individual rather than with relationship, leaving the object of knowledge bereft of any intrinsic value other than what we may assign to it. We have lost the sense of knowledge as experience, and we need to find it anew. In an essay entitled, "How to Love a Worm?" friar and biologist Jim Edmiston sought to understand the fly he was studying not by observation and measurement but by entering the world of the fly:

> After I saw the world from the perspective of a fly larva, the world never looked the same. Each living creature becomes an instrument of creation that cries out to be respected for its role and for its individuality. Species no longer become

abstractions, but realities to be lived through each unique life in each unique moment of time. Connecting with as many of these life forms as possible has changed me into a person who not only continues to explore the diversity of life, but also is able to reverence the creator through appreciation of the individuals who constitute the diversity.[2]

British anthropologist Gregory Bateson in his *Steps to an Ecology of Mind* criticized our Western form of knowledge because it is too linear and does not account for the interplay of consciousness. He described the individual, society, and ecosystem as part of one large cybernetic system which he called the Mind. We know things within the larger realm of consciousness not as objects outside ourselves but interrelated to ourselves. Only when thought and emotion are combined are we able to obtain complete knowledge; that is, knowledge belongs as much to the body as to the mind.[3]

Knowledge is to deepen our participation in the whole, not to control it. When we are unconscious of our connectedness to the world of things, we cannot be intelligently related to them. We know objects as data not as mirrors of reflection. The self that is divorced from the world of conscious experience is a self that tries to control the world. One knows intellectually but not intelligently; from a part of the brain but not the whole person; from the mind but not from the heart. Such knowledge does not deepen a person as a relational being but isolates and individualizes.

Our modern educational system is based on the self-thinking subject. The world is a collection of objects that the self encounters. As it experiences these objects, the self must organize the experiences to make sense of the world. Hence the meaning of the world, as it begins in the self-thinking self, terminates in the same self.

Knowledge is taken from the object of encounter as a product for individual gain. One consumes the information of experience, takes it in, chews it up and spits it out without necessarily being changed by it. Consumptive knowledge can lead to individual power without regard for the inherent good of the other, leading to manipulation of peoples, nations, and the planet of finite resources.

Bonaventure and Wisdom Theology

While love is key to a sustainable future, and through love a widened sense of compassion, we need to rediscover the link between knowledge and love which is wisdom. Wisdom is knowledge deepened by love. It is a penetrating vision into the heart of things by which one knows in a way more deeply than the mind alone can grasp. Wisdom is found in the experience of the sacred. It brings to light the depths of things that simultaneously reveal and veil the divine mystery.

Bonaventure uses the word *perscrutatio* to describe the knowing process that leads to wisdom, "searching through" the known, allowing the depth of the mystery to unveil itself without destroying it.[4] The theologian who is a *perscrutator* is like a treasure hunter—a seeker of pearls—who fathoms the unsuspected depths of the divine mystery, searching out its inmost hiding places and revealing its most beautiful jewels.[5] Bonaventure indicates that when God expresses something of his Trinitarian grandeur, it is then left to the theologian to search it out or penetrate it insofar as one allows oneself to be inhabited by the wisdom of God which alone brings all things to light.[6] This idea plays out in the life of Francis of Assisi who, filled with the Holy Spirit, contemplated God's overflowing love in creation.

Emmanual Falque writes that to discover the hidden order of divine wisdom is not only to search the depths of God in himself but "the depth of God hidden in his created works in which and by which he justly manifests his wisdom."[7] Bonaventure describes Francis as the true *perscrutator* through the act of contuition which is a grasp of something in itself and simultaneously in God.

Bonaventure's "method" redirects the novelty of its approach toward the internal disposition of the subject which alone can explain it. The searcher of divine depths must be on the journey to God; that is, only one filled with the Spirit can search the depths of God. For Bonaventure, there is no purely speculative conceptual determination. To make the manifestation of God into a purely speculative act creates confusion. Rather, theology is to make God manifest so as to orient one toward an encounter through love between God and his act of revelation and the human person in one's affective power. Love therefore becomes a conceptual determination at the junction of theory and practice. Falque writes, "any strictly theological truth, one that has its roots in God, will no longer be content with its unique objective determination." Such a truth, Falque states, "will take on a performative sense, one that is transforming for the subject that states it, or it will not exist.... Knowledge through love is the only thing that puts in motion whoever comes to know them."[8]

Wisdom is the principle of true knowledge. It is light, mirror, exemplar, and book of life; it is "utterly simple and perfect" and therefore can arise from no other than God.[9] Wisdom belongs uniquely to the Word of God; as the *medium* of the Trinity, the Word lies between the Father and Spirit, rendering order and unity to the Trinity. In creation, the crucified Word is the revelation of God's wisdom where God reaches down to the depths of the world and draws all things back to himself. Bonaventure states that wisdom is an experiential knowledge of God that begins with contemplation or a vision of God as the source of all created reality and culminates in "tasting God" which is a union of love that is *agapic* or compassionate. Wisdom is the most excellent gift of the Holy Spirit and unites the soul with Christ through contemplation. As Bonaventure points out in his spiritual writings, one does not attain wisdom through effort alone, but one acquires wisdom through the gifts of the Holy Spirit.[10]

Wisdom bears many fruits including recognition of one's inner defects, control of the passions, ordaining of thoughts, and elevation of desire. The gift of wisdom from above is the light which descends to illuminate our cognitive potency to gladden our affective potency and to fortify our operative potency. Bonaventure speaks of wisdom as a certain disposition of the soul, a *habitus*, by which the mind can apprehend the wisdom of God.

Although wisdom has several forms which Bonaventure describes in his second collation on the *Hexaëmeron*, the highest form of wisdom, contemplative wisdom, entails a love that transcends all understanding and knowledge, a "formless wisdom" (*sapientia nulliformis*). This wisdom of God, he claims, "is mysterious, hidden... which...eye has not seen nor ear heard, nor has it entered into the heart of man.... But to us God has revealed [it] through His Spirit. For the Spirit searches all things, even the deep things of God." [11] This is the wisdom of the *perscrutator*, which is attained through the grace of contemplation and the supreme union of love. "Such love," according to Bonaventure, "transcends every intellect and science." [12] "In this union," he continues, "the mind is joined to God, wherefore in a certain sense it sleeps.... Only the affective power keeps vigil and imposes silence upon all the other powers."[13] To plumb the depths of mystical theology, for Bonaventure, is to attain wisdom or that highest union in love which is an experiential and thus more perfect knowledge of God marked by silence and death. Bonaventure writes:

Now such love divides, puts to sleep, and lifts up. It divides, since it cuts away from any other love because of the single love for the Spouse; it puts to sleep and appeases all the powers and imposes silence; it lifts up, since it leads to God. And so man is dead, where it is said: *Love is strong as death* (Corinthians 8:6), because it cuts away from all things. Man, then, must die of this love in order to be lifted up.[14]

The metaphors of sleep, silence, and death indicate that this highest form of wisdom comes about through transformation in the cross. The cross is the disclosure of God's wisdom in a formless form, symbolized by the death of Christ. What appears fragile and broken is the outpouring love of the Trinity; the shattering of Christ's body is the release of the costly ointment of divine wisdom. Although God's wisdom is light, it is revealed in darkness, silence, suffering, and death. Only one who is conformed to the Crucified through poverty and humility can see this light because one participates, through imitation of Christ, in the fragile form of God's self-involving love. One must be on the spiritual journey to know the depths of God's love expressed in the depths of the cross. That is, one cannot *know* God in himself but as God *reveals* Godself; one must *experience* God, for the Trinity is incomprehensible love beyond which our intelligence can perceive. Bonaventure writes: "Christ goes away when the mind attempts to behold this wisdom through intellectual eyes; since it is not the intellect that can go in there, but the heart."[15] The wisdom of the cross is the wisdom of God which shatters all other forms of knowledge and opens one up to the depth of mystery. One must be transformed into the love of the Crucified to enter into what is disclosed as lasting and true.

It is this type of knowledge that led Francis of Assisi to a renewed sense of the sacred in creation. Thomas of Celano said of Francis:

Where the knowledge of teachers is outside,
the passion of the lover entered.
He sometimes read the Sacred Books,
and whatever he once put into his mind,
he *wrote* indelibly *in his heart.*
His memory took the place of books,
Because if his heart heard something once,
it was not wasted,
as his heart would mull it over with constant devotion.[16]

The spiritual person who has surrendered to love and whose heart is moved by love sees the world as rich in goodness. Bonaventure wrote of Francis that when he encountered living creatures he called them "sister" and "brother" because he recognized that they shared the same source of primordial goodness as himself.[17] Francis approached creatures as a poor brother, as one dispossessed and related. This is quite different from the modern person who approaches others as one who is self-possessed. Is it possible for the modern person to attain a reorientation of being and knowing in the world?

Francis' compassion was grounded in his depth of vision. As he shifted from his egocentrism to a relational self through the deepening of love, he released control of his life and the lives of others. His knowledge and freedom became deep and wide enough to invite others into his life. Francis grew into an ecological person because he grew into a God-centered person. His "biophilia" began with the poor, the sick, the weak and fragile, and as he grew in relationship with them, he came to know God in a new way. He accepted the

leper as a brother, as one he was related to, and this acceptance broad-
ened his relatedness to others. The weak and fragile creatures of the
earth spoke to him most clearly of the presence of Christ. Thomas of
Celano writes:

> Even for worms he had a warm love, since he had read this
> text about the Savior: *I am a worm and not a man.* That is why
> he used to pick them up from the road and put them in a safe
> place so that they would not be crushed by the footsteps of
> passersby.
>
> ...
>
> Whenever he found an abundance of flowers, he used to
> preach to them and invite them to praise the Lord, just as if
> they were endowed with reason.[18]
> That the bees not perish of hunger in the icy winter, he
> commands that honey and the finest wine should be set out
> for them.
> He calls all animals by a fraternal name, although, among
> all kinds of beasts, he especially loves the meek.[19]

Compassion shows itself in care for the other; it is not mere senti-
ment but a sense of responsibility to strengthen the weak and lift up
the fallen by creating a space of support and comfort. For Francis, all
creatures became his family. He saw goodness throughout the whole
cosmic creation and found himself as part of this creation; not above
it but within it. His entire life was an integration of knowledge and
love, spirit and matter, divinity and humanity. He held together the
opposites of life by living in the unity of love.

In the year 1225 the year before his death, Francis composed one
of the most beautiful poems in the Umbrian dialect. What is most

striking about the poem is its genesis. He had lived a harsh life, renouncing the pleasures of the body, and lived as a wandering hermit and servant of the poor. He spent most of his life among lepers, eating scraps of food periodically and denying his body the warmth of material goods. By the year 1225 his body was worn out. Blind, leprous, and suffering from a gastrointestinal disorder, Francis lay sick in a small hut behind the convent of San Damiano where his companion Clare of Assisi lived with her religious sisters. His eye condition had deteriorated to such an extent that the physical light of day caused intense pain. He had to remain in darkness. He had reached the point of physical exhaustion; yet deep inside him a voice spoke, asking if his sufferings were worth an earth transformed in gold. Upon this insight he awoke and sang the "Canticle of the Creatures" and in doing so expressed the harmony of the universe that lay deep within him.

The sense of family that Francis attained with creation was not merely superficial but rather reflected a new vision of reality. The words "brother" and "sister" were words of mystery for Francis, so graphically did they disclose to him the structure of reality. The "Canticle" is a hymn of praise that recapitulates Francis' journey to God in and through creation which became for him a *theophany*, a manifestation of God.

But the "Canticle" also represents a lifetime of conversion, as Francis strove to be a brother to all things, despite his sufferings, feelings of abandonment and darkness. In this hymn of celebration to the cosmic Christ (although not explicitly named), Francis addresses the "Most High," the ineffable God who has become flesh.[20] He speaks of the mystery of Jesus Christ through the metaphor of "Brother Sun." The words "Most High" and "humility" which begin and end the "Canticle" symbolically enclose the whole universe in a cosmic

Incarnation.[21] It is "Brother Sun" who is "the day and through whom [God] gives us light" who is at center of the cosmos, that light which is the splendor and glory of the Father. Francis' praises of God are notes of joy resounding throughout the universe. He sings:

> *Praised* be You, my Lord, through Sister *Moon* and *the stars*,
> in heaven You formed them clear and precious and
>   beautiful.
> Praised be You, my Lord, through Brother Wind,
> and through the air, cloudy and serene, and every kind of
>   weather,
> through whom You give sustenance to Your creatures.
> *Praised* be You, my Lord, through Sister *Water*,
> who is very useful and humble and precious and chaste.
> *Praised* be You, my Lord, through Brother *Fire*,
> through whom *You light the night*,
> and he is beautiful and playful and robust and strong.
> *Praised* be You, my Lord, through our Sister Mother *Earth*,
> who sustains and governs us,
> and who produces various *fruit* with colored flowers and
>   herbs.[22]

Like the three youths in the fiery furnace (Daniel 3:57–90), Francis praises God "through" (*per*) the elements of creation, for the "Canticle" discloses Francis' view of nature as a sacramental expression of God's generous love. This love binds us together in a family of relationships that are rightly termed "brother" and "sister." Francis acquired a "vision" of cosmic interdependency in and through his relation to Christ. Through his love of Christ crucified he came to see the truth of reality, namely, that nothing exists autonomously and independently;

rather everything is related to each other. The "Canticle" expresses Francis' interior life transformed in Christ and projects that interior life onto the cosmos where Christ is the center of reality.[23] It is like a cosmic liturgy in which Christ is the high Priest. Through him, with him, and in him, everything is offered up in praise to the glory of the Father, in the love of the Holy Spirit.[24] Just as Christ became the center of Francis' own life, so too Francis realized that Christ is the center of creation.

The "Canticle" reminds us that we humans are as dependent on the elements of creation as they are dependent on us. With his marvelous respect for creatures of all kinds, for sun, moon, stars, water, wind, fire, and earth, Francis came to see that all creation gives praise to God. Brother Sun and Sister Moon praise God just by being sun and moon.[25] We might say that Francis became sensitive to the goodness of creation so that he came to understand, hear, and see the sun and moon praising God. The "Canticle" foreshadows the new creation where we will find ourselves related to all things of creation in a spirit of reconciliation and peace.[26] It brings to our awareness that the entire creation is charged with the goodness of God. All creation gives praise and glory to the Most High; it is the sacrament of God.

As the final song of his life, the "Canticle" reveals to us Francis' deep reflection on the mystery of God in creation. Creation and Incarnation are intimately united in such a way that we cannot truly grasp our relationship to creation apart from our relationship to God. The deeper he grew in relationship with Christ, the more he found himself intimately related to the things of creation as brother. We might say that his relationship with the divine mystery changed his internal focus. He developed a deeper consciousness of "relatedness" and came to realize he was related to all things, no matter how small, because everything shared in the primordial goodness of God who is the source of his life's abundance. Francis discovered his place in the cosmos; not as center but as brother.

The "Canticle of Creatures" is the way the universe looks after the ego has disappeared. It is a vision of the whole that sees the self as part of the whole in the unity of love. The way to this vision for Francis was compassion. His life was an ever-widening space in union with the divine, a space between God and Francis that included the leper, the sick brother, the sun, moon, and stars. Francis saw the world within the divine embrace. He felt the tender love of God shining through creation. His "Canticle of Creatures" sings of compassion, a unity in love with everything in creation. Each element bears immense dignity, and no element of creation, no matter how small, is insignificant. Light shines through the most humble of creatures because divine compassion is the luminous thread that binds all together in love.

Meditation

Wisdom is knowledge deepened by love. The wise person is one whose heart has been shaped by love and who has given one's heart to love.

For Reflection

1. Try to find a quiet place outdoors and sit quietly for five minutes. Be attentive to what is in your mind and heart; and what is present to you. Then, slowly pray the "Canticle of Creatures" (see page 88).
2. In the next few days, try to write your own "Canticle."
3. How does the root of Francis' ecological stance begin with his encounter with God and his conversion toward the divine? How do you relate this to your own conversion story?

4. Francis' compassion was grounded in his depth of vision. How do you share that vision of compassion?

5. Compare the verses of the "Canticle of Creatures" with our current economy and global reality. Read the "Canticle" after taking the online ecological footprint quiz http://myfootprint.org.

6. What can we learn from Francis' "Canticle" that can make a difference in our world today?

Cyberspace and Compassion

| We live in an age of virtual reality. It is an unprecedented age in human history and certainly one very different from the age of Francis. What makes it so different is not just the influx of technology into daily life but the new self that is now an extension of technology. Try throwing out your cell phone, disconnecting your computer, putting away your iPod and going into the wilderness, and you will confront someone who will seem like a stranger, namely, yourself. Daily human life is so intertwined with technology that it is sometimes difficult to see where the human ends and technology begins. In its various forms, technology is changing the human person. Noreen Herzfeld writes:

> In today's world, technology is central to our understanding of ourselves and the environment around us.... But technology plays an undeniably greater role in our lives than it has at any previous time in human history.
>
> That greater role is also seen in the power to create something new,... To create the new is to go outside of nature... the German existentialist Martin Heidegger observes that the ancient craftsman certainly made something new when

he constructed a chair. A doctor might bring new health to a patient. However, neither imposed a new form on nature; rather, each worked with what is already implicit in the wood or the body.... The new products of modern technology do not simply "disclose" or shape nature but transform and replace nature. In this way, modern technology gives us heretofore undreamed of power.[1]

The development of artificial intelligence (A.I.) is of particular interest because it centers on devices such as computers and robots associated with human intelligence. Although A.I. has its proximate roots in the British mathematician Alan Turing who believed that a thinking machine could be made to mimic human intelligence, its more distal roots are in René Descartes's *cogito ergo sum* and the priority of the mental over the material.

In 1950 Turing developed a test in which a computer was set up to fool judges into believing that it could be human. The test was performed by conducting a text-based conversation on a subject. If the computer's responses were indistinguishable from those of a human, it had passed the Turing test and could be said to be "thinking." John McCarthy coined the term "artificial intelligence" in 1956, defining it as "the science and engineering of making intelligent machines." Because artificial intelligence mimics human intelligence, it expresses our ability to create ourselves through intelligent machines. But is the image we share with God the same image we wish to share with our technological creations? Herzfeld writes: "The way we define God's image in our human nature or our image in the computer has implications, not only for how we view ourselves but also for how we relate to God, to one another, and to our own creations."[2]

Since World War II, the mechanization of the human, the vitalization of the machine, and the integration of both into cybernetics has produced a whole new range of informational disciplines, fantasies, and practices that have transgressed the mechanical-organic border.[3] This influx of technology into daily life has transformed our patterns of play, work, love, birth, sickness, and death.

The word *cyborg* is a term of and for our times that maps contemporary bodily and social reality as a hybrid of biology and machine. A *cyborg* is a person whose physiological functioning is aided by or dependent on a mechanical or electronic device. In a more general sense, cyborg refers "to creatures that are both organic and technological."[4] An increasing number of people are becoming "cyborged" in the technical sense, including people with electronic pacemakers, artificial joints, drug implant systems, implanted corneal lenses, and artificial skin. The integration of technology in daily human life around the globe has rendered us technologically-dependent beings in which technology has come to organize daily life.

The *cyborg* is becoming the interpretive symbol for the human self because the cybernetic loop generates a new kind of subjectivity. Some scholars lament the enlarging role of machines in human socialization. The philosophical and religious heritage of the West, according to Naomi Goldenberg, leaves Westerners predisposed to form harmful attitudes toward the technologies overtaking their lives. This heritage has taught us that human life is a rough copy of something out there— something better, wiser, and purer.[5] As a result, Westerners possess a cultural proclivity to respond to machines not as tools to use but as role models to emulate. As people act upon this proclivity, she states, the isolation and loneliness of modern life are being increased. We are becoming more comfortable with machines than with people.

It is not surprising that the rapid success of *cyborgs* corresponds to advancements in embodied artificial intelligence, especially in the area of robotics. Although the engineering required for humanoid robotics lags behind the progress of A.I., both efforts seek the creation of intelligent mechanical life. Recent studies on robotics indicate that robots will be integrated into the human community within the next fifty years.[6] At MIT, for example, researchers are building robots as embodied entities (such as Cog and Kismet) that interact with their real environments, including emotional responses. Robots are already incorporated into the industrial world. One company, RobotWorx, states that "machine loading robots increase productivity, which in turn increases revenue."[7] The futurist Ray Kurzweil anticipates an increasingly virtual life in which the bodily presence of human beings will become irrelevant. Robert Jastrow of NASA believes that "human evolution is nearly a finished chapter in the history of life," although the evolution of intelligence will not end because a new species will arise, "a new kind of intelligent life more likely to be made of silicon."[8] Katherine Hayles claims that artificial intelligence is forming a new type of posthuman species where there are no essential differences between bodily existence and computer simulation, cybernetic mechanism and biological organism, robot technology and human goals.[9] We will eventually become like the dinosaurs, she says, a species that once ruled the earth but is now obsolete. In her view, the age of the human is drawing to a close.[10]

Transhumanists look to a post-biological future where super informational beings will flourish and biological limits such as disease, aging, and death, and perhaps even sin, will be overcome. Kurzweil anticipates an increasingly virtual life in which the bodily presence of human beings will become irrelevant because of artificial intelligence.

He claims that machine-dependent humans will transcend death through the virtual reality of eternal life, possibly by "neurochips" or simply by becoming totally machine dependent.

As we move beyond mortality through computational technology, our identity will be based on our evolving mind file. We will be software, not hardware. By replacing living bodies with virtual bodies capable of transferral and duplication, we will become disembodied superminds.[11] Robert Geraci states, "our new selves will be infinitely replicable, allowing them to escape the finality of death."[12] This futuristic "post-biological" computer-based immortality is also envisioned by Hans Moravec who claims that the advent of intelligent machines (*machina sapiens*) will provide humanity with personal immortality by mind transplant. Moravec suggests that the mind will be able to be downloaded into a machine through the eventual replacement of brain cells by electronic circuits and identical input-output functions.[13] Daniel Crevier argues that A.I. is consistent with the Christian belief in resurrection and immortality. Since some kind of support is required for the information and organization that constitutes our minds, Crevier indicates, a material, mechanical replacement for the mortal body will suffice. "Christ was resurrected in a new body," he states, "why not a machine?"[14]

Margaret Wertheim notes that artificial intelligence is spawning a philosophical shift, from reality constructed of matter and energy to reality constructed of information.[15] Books such as *Digital Being* point in the same direction: Information has come to define reality. This leads to the notion that "the essence of a person can be separated from their body and represented in digital form—an immortal digital soul waiting to be freed—an idea she [Wertheim] sees as medieval dualism reincarnated."[16] A new term, *cybergnosticism*, has been coined

to describe the "belief that the physical world is impure or ineffi-
cient, and that existence in the form of pure information is better
and should be pursued."[17] Michael Heim sees strong links between
artificial intelligence and Platonic, Gnostic, and Hermetic traditions
insofar as they emphasize the goodness of spiritual reality and cor-
ruption of material reality, an idea consonant with cyber life and post-
humanism. Heim writes:

> Cyberspace is Platonism as a working product. The cyber-
> naut seated before us, strapped into sensory-input devices,
> appears to be, and is indeed, lost to this world. Suspended in
> computer space, the cybernaut leaves the prison of the body
> and emerges in a world of digital sensation.[18]

The myth of technology is appealing and the power of technology is
seductive. We now have the power not only to evolve ourselves but to
direct the course of evolution. Whereas in biological evolution nature
influences or mutually interacts with the species, in technological evolution, species controls nature. In the human person biological evolution has become technological evolution, and evolution has become
directed toward a new, emerging posthuman species, *techno sapiens*.

However, a posthuman world is ultimately a postnatural world.
While artificial intelligence aims toward a new virtual body, it also
anticipates a new virtual creation where the earthly garden will eventually wither away and be replaced by a much greater world, a paradise
never to be lost.[19] Through mechanical means we will soon be able to
overcome the limitations of the body, including suffering and death,
and thus attain artificial eschatological paradise—or so the masters of
artificial intelligence prophesy.

Artificial Compassion?

The influx of technology in daily life leads us to ask: Is technology altering our sense of compassion? In Francis' time the feeling of compassion meant the personal experience of another's suffering, the felt experience of pain which meant knowing the other not just as an idea but a bodily human person; the flesh embodied spirit. When Francis met the leper he saw, tasted, touched, kissed the leper's ulcerous hand and in this experience of the leper's weak flesh, he tasted the goodness of God. Compassion is the feeling of sympathy evoked by the vision of another's suffering. What happens to compassion in virtual reality, when an individual can control connections online? Is compassion possible in a controlled world? Or does compassion require the uncontrolled and uncontrollable encounter with another human person or living creature?

In an essay on biomedical technology, ethicist Ronald Cole-Turner states that technologies today "are self-asserting rather than self-transforming, enhancing the ego rather than surrendering it to a greater reality and purpose."[20] Artificial intelligence is not simply a desire to live an alternate life in a cyber world, he states, but a desire to perfect and control our imperfect lives. The lure of technology is that it "offers the illusion of a managed grace"; the self that can fix itself up without changing itself.[21] Is virtual compassion, whether by robot or online, really compassion if it leaves the self unchanged?

When we reflect on Francis' encounter with the leper, we are struck not only by his acceptance of the leper but more so that Francis himself was changed in the encounter. If compassion is the response of the heart to suffering, then it is also the capacity of the heart to embrace suffering and be changed by it. Francis' compassion was not intellectual but experiential, the experience of knowing another's misery. Thomas of Celano writes:

Great was his compassion towards the sick and great his concern for their needs. If lay people's piety sent him tonics he would give it to the others who were sick even though he had greater need of them. He had sympathy for all who were ill and when he could not alleviate their pain he offered words of compassion. He would eat on fast days so the weak would not be ashamed of eating, and he was not embarrassed to go through the city's public places to find some meat for a sick brother.[22]

My mother used to say that growing up in the Great Depression was a better time than in the late twentieth century when wealth and success became more common. During the Depression, she said, people were concerned for one another and would share their limited resources so that the poorer members of the community would not be denied their basic needs. Although the struggles of the Great Depression were great, love did conquer fear.

A number of years ago I took a mission trip to El Salvador, and we visited a small village up in the mountains. The people were poor, but their hospitality was magnificent. Standing on the thresholds of open doors they invited us into to their one-room homes that held everything from the motorcycle to the kitchen sink. They were not concerned about appearance or whether or not we would invade their privacy. Rather, they extended themselves in friendship and hospitality to a group of weary pilgrims. They saw our need for respite and invited us into their homes.

The problem of virtual reality is personal reality. Technology allows us to alter the real or to create the real according to our desires. Technology promises a world liberated from suffering and death, a world devoid of the wild and unpredictable. Richard Louv states that nature means "natural wildness, biodiversity and abundance."[23] It serves as a blank slate upon which a child draws and reinterprets the culture's fantasies, a creation that is somehow richer than the scientifically accessible world, because it interacts more intimately with a person. A thoroughly domesticated nature can no longer fulfill this role. When the artificiality of a random number algorithm, such as a computer game, replaces the surprises of natural richness, we lose something of human life. We lose the sense of what it means to be created, dependent, contingent and finite. "Nature offers healing... but it can frighten...and this fright serves a purpose, to awaken in us our dependency on God, the earth and other people."[24] Alfred Kracher says that a "planet ruled by predictability," where "all contingency has been eliminated," is also a planet "dominated by unchecked evil."[25] If we can control our relationships, our loves, and our dislikes, we may not only control evil unwittingly, but we may become evil unknowingly.

Technology that operates on individual control preempts relationships of dependency on one another and the earth. Artificial intelligence can offer community without commitment, mutuality without responsibility. It can lend itself to narcissism, self-indulgence, and isolation. Herzfeld indicates that video games today may be reinforcing violent behavior in teenagers. She describes the prevalence of violent video games among teenage boys where one can play in the "god mode," controlling life and death. She indicates that playing violent video games may be rewiring the human brain or at least enhancing those brain centers associated with violence and aggressive behavior.[26] I do not know of any online game of compassion, but I suspect that such a game would not be popular, since it would lack the thrill of violence to which our culture is addicted.

Transhumanists look to a post-biological world, a garden of online happiness free of suffering and death, threatening to sacrifice the organic whole at the expense of perfecting the human. The very human limitations we want to eliminate, however—suffering and death—are the most important elements for the evolution of life. By artificially trying to control our destiny we cut ourselves off from the richness of life. We prevent others from really entering our lives by interfacing our relationships with artificial devices.

The type of knowledge that leads to compassion is more than information. The pain of the other must touch a center deep within us, and we in turn must act out of a center that seeks more than rational reason or self-gratification. The act of compassion through the interplay of love, experience, touch, and vision is a deep experience of life by which one crosses the threshold of separateness to enter into union.

This act of crossing a threshold was recently illustrated in a televised drama of a woman suffering from kidney failure. Three times a week she had to go for treatment, and each time she sat across from a middle-aged man who refused to talk to her. One day she decided she would sit next to him for her treatment, and while he resented her nearness, she persisted. They sat quietly together, and after some time she reached over and took his hand into hers—and he began to weep. Her eyes of compassion could see the fear deep within him. "To acknowledge and cross a new threshold is always a challenge," the poet John O'Donohue writes:

> It demands courage and also a sense of trust in whatever is emerging. This becomes essential when a threshold opens suddenly in front of you, one for which you had no preparation. This could be illness, suffering, or loss. Because we are

so engaged with the world, we usually forget how fragile life can be and how vulnerable we always are. It takes only a couple of seconds for a life to change irreversibly. Suddenly you stand on completely strange ground and a new course of life has to be embraced. Especially at such times we desperately need blessing and protection. You look back at the life you have lived up to a few hours before, and it suddenly seems so far away. Think for a moment how, across the world, someone's life has just changed—irrevocably, permanently, and not necessarily for the better—and everything that was once so steady, so reliable, must now find a new way of unfolding.[27]

If we are to live compassionately today, then we need to feel the pulse of life in the concrete pain of existence. We need hearts that *feel* for another and the patience of slowed time to be for another. Love can create a field of compassion, but love requires mutuality. Technology may virtually unite us, but love transforms us, and love alone will deepen our humanity.

Meditation
If we can control our relationships, our loves and our dislikes, we not only control evil unwittingly, but we can become evil unknowingly.

For Reflection
1. What thoughts and feelings come to mind as you consider the possibility of living in a "posthuman" world? Who will be included in this world? Who will be excluded or left out from this "posthuman" world?

2. Given what you know about Francis of Assisi, what do you think is an appropriate Franciscan response to the world of cyber reality?

3. How can we effectively negotiate our way in a technological world so that we do not sacrifice our sense of connection with others?

4. What steps can we take to strengthen a sense of connectedness and compassion with others—including not only family and friends, but even strangers we meet in public?

5. What are some ways that we can be more "present" to those strangers we encounter in public places?

6. Practice a cyberfast one day a week for four weeks. Reflect on this fast and your practice of compassion.

Community

| There is a new longing for community in the twenty-first century. The independent Baby Boomer generation is entering retirement, and upcoming generations such as Gen X and Gen Y show signs of desiring to belong to a whole. Sociologists note a complexity of factors spawning this new interest in community life, including the rise of the ecological movement, online venues such as Facebook and Twitter, the dissipation of family life, and the feeling of loneliness in modern society.

But we might also see the new interest in community life related to the new scientific worldview of a thoroughly relational universe. The discovery of evolution in the nineteenth century and quantum physics in the twentieth century are the two pillars of modern science. Evolution tells us that life unfolds from simple to complex structures over long periods of time through chance and law. We live in a mid-sized galaxy in an evolutionary universe that is about 13.7 billion years old with billions of other galaxies; a universe that is large, dynamic, and interconnected. It is not a fixed, static, immutable universe but more like an expanding balloon. In this long unfolding story of the universe, we humans are the last two words—*homo sapiens sapiens*; we know that we know. We are the evolutionary universe become conscious of itself.

In the first decade of the twentieth century, Albert Einstein's discovery of relativity changed our understanding of absolute space and time, uprooting the Newtonian mechanistic universe. Quantum physics tells us that the world is nothing like it appears; it is a world of probabilities rather than certainties, interconnected to the core.

Community is what the universe is about, and if one were to ask the sun, the moon, and the stars what is the reason for their beauty, they would probably answer, "We live as community in compassion." There is synergy among the elements of the universe; the ecological world is primarily a cooperative one. A number of years ago the biologist Lewis Thomas wrote a book called *The Lives of a Cell: Notes from a Biology Watcher*. He noted that the whole earth functions like a living cell, each part something of the whole, cooperating with other parts to maintain the whole.

In the 1960s James Lovelock formulated the Gaia hypothesis to describe the biosphere and physical components of the planet Earth (atmosphere, cryosphere, hydrosphere, and lithosphere) as closely integrated, indicating the Earth has its own regulating mechanisms to keep it in balance.[1] Nature is a family that stays together. When one part is injured, another part steps in to help the cause. Frans de Waal, the noted primatologist, has found that some primates exhibit moral behavior that mirrors compassion. Bonobos, for example, "share food, show a strong sense of right and wrong and exhibit feelings of shame, guilt, sympathy and concern."[2] Tijn Touber tells the story of a three-year-old boy "who fell 18 feet into the primate enclosure at Chicago's Brookfield Zoo. A gorilla named Binti Jua picked up the child and carried him to safety. She sat down on a log and rocked the boy on her lap, patting him a few times on his back, before taking him to waiting zoo staff. Her show of sympathy, captured on video

and shown around the world, touched many hearts."[3] The studies on
primate behavior sheds light on biological solidarity. Compassion
between nonhuman and human transcends the boundaries of species
and shows how deeply related we are.

Compassion and Community

While the natural world does much better at living cooperatively and
compassionately, it is much more difficult on the human level. The
development of the human ego as a protective center can mushroom
into a hard shell that does not let the true self out or other selves
in too readily. Compassion needs relationship because it is solidarity
of the heart. Without real relationship, compassion cannot flourish.
When Francis saw the weakness of another creature, he saw the passion of Christ, and his heart was deeply moved to love the creature as
his kin. Thomas of Celano wrote that he loved tenderly, including the
most humble beings of nature:

> He spares lanterns, lamps, and candles unwilling to use his
> hand to put out their brightness which is a sign of the *eternal
> light*. He walks reverently over rocks, out of respect for Him
> who is called *the Rock*...
>
> When the brothers are cutting wood he forbids them
> to cut down the whole tree, so that it might have hope of
> sprouting again... He picks up little worms from the road so
> they will not be trampled underfoot... He calls all animals
> by a fraternal name, although, among all kinds of beasts, he
> especially loves the meek.[4]

When Francis saw a poor person, he would often give away his mantle
or some goods to the person. One time a poor woman who had two
sons in religious life came to the friary to seek alms. Because the

friars had nothing to give the poor woman, Francis gave her the New Testament book (a rare and expensive item in those days) so she could sell it and obtain the money for her needs.[5] His mercy and compassion were as limitless as the overflowing love of God.

Charles Eisenstein notes that community is nearly impossible in a highly monetized society like our own. "There are many reasons" he writes, "the layout of suburbia, the disappearance of public space, the automobile and the television, the high mobility of people and jobs—and, if you trace the 'why's' a few levels down, they all implicate the money system."[6] Francis discovered this truth in his own time. Seeing how financial wealth can preclude the needs of others, he disowned his father's patrimony and gave all that he had to the poor. He *made himself* dependent on others.

Eisenstein points to the same reality in our time. When money creates independence, the neighbor becomes an infringement on our time, and we prefer our private space to public communal events. We do not *need* others, and thus we choose to live in our own private worlds.

Today, the substitution of money for personal relationships has had deleterious results not only on the human community but on the earth community as well. Our energy supplies are diminishing, global warming continues to heat the earth, the industrialization of food is costing us ecologically and nutritionally, and the poor are suffering these catastrophes disproportionately. When success means to be better off than your neighbors in a society based on money, the whole is bound for self-destruction because living beings are disposable means rather than inviolable ends.[7] Human beings become disconnected from one another and the whole earth is undone. The disconnected human person lives in fear that he or she will be reduced to nothing if all material wealth is lost. Hence the goods of the earth are coveted, space becomes a commodity, and community is broken.

Compassion is another name for community. Francis called the brothers to love each other as a mother loves her son because anything else can become self-absorbing. To be compassionate one must be related to others and to see others as a mirror of oneself; hence it is closely tied with contemplation. Recent brain studies have shown that compassion may be hard wired in the brain. We are wired to respond and help others in need. Some scientists suggest that the brain has mirror neurons. When we encounter a person in need or distress or we imagine what their experience is like, our neurons detect pain in the other, and a feeling of empathy impels us to act for another person's welfare, even at our own expense.

Dacher Keltner notes that brain structures involved in the positive emotions like compassion are more plastic and subject to changes brought about by environmental input. We might think about compassion as a biologically based skill or virtue that can be cultivated in the appropriate context.[8] Positive environments that enforce a feeling of love and protection enhance the practice of compassion while negative environments of hostility or fear cause greater competition and aggressiveness at the expense of compassion. The key, it seems, lies in the relational nature of being itself. When positive relationships promote a greater sense of self, compassion shows itself more readily in the desire to maintain the good in oneself and others. When relationships are negative or disconnected, the feeling of isolation or the fear of loss impels one to aggressively compete against another, seizing the good of the other for the sake of oneself.

Sometimes we can be so preoccupied with ourselves that we are blind to the world around us. Our hearts become hardened from the layers of self-absorption we wrap around them. How do we break open our hardened hearts and welcome the God of the suffering neighbor into our midst?

Compassion requires conversion because unless we become other-centered rather than self-centered, we cannot see the truth in our midst. Prayerful conversion is openness to grace that allows one to be at home with oneself, turning from self-centeredness toward God-centeredness. The Greek work for conversion, *metanoia*, means "the shifting of minds," the way one sees a situation in a new way. Francis saw the awesome mystery of God in the disfigured leper; his way of life was a "heart to heart" encounter. Engagement with the other was at the same time engagement with God. The focus of his life was out of the self and toward the other, a "being with" in compassion. He learned to pray with a penetrating gaze that could see the truth of reality. His contemplative being in the world was a compassionate being for others. By entering compassionately into the experience of the other, he could penetrate beyond the appearance all the way down to reality, to the truth of the other in contemplation.

Compassion and Patience

Compassion requires patience. We often place unnecessary demands on ourselves and on others. When we are not open to the grace of God or fail to see God's grace in the ordinary events of our lives, we can set unreasonable expectations for ourselves and others. We want to be something God has no knowledge of, and we want others to be something they are not capable of. God can do nothing for us because we refuse to let God live in us. In some ways, we are like walking zombies who consume the earth and all its resources, unconscious of other living creatures. We covet the goods of others as if they belong to us. Self-absorbed creatures are impatient and intolerant of others because they are intolerant of themselves. The neighbor becomes an intrusion and life is a burden. The person who lives alone dies alone because they refuse to love.

Compassion requires us to let go and let God shine through weak matter. That is why compassion is difficult online. How does one allow the suffering of another to enter into the heart when the human face is constructed on a light emitting diode screen? Howard Rheingold states that "people in virtual communities. . . do just about everything people do in real life, but we leave our bodies behind."[9]

There is something both right and wrong today with regard to social network communities. The heart yearns to give itself away, but it also fears that in giving itself away, it may get hurt, trampled on, or lost. The artificial medium of the iPhone or computer provides a safe space to share one's life without having to deal with rejection. As I already discussed, technology binds us together while keeping us apart. The human person may be able to meet his or her emotional, spiritual, and psychological needs online, but can one grow as a person?

When we can control our relationships, for example, by rejecting our friends on Facebook or refusing to answer e-mails or phone calls, we have no place for the grace of conversion because we have no room for others in our lives. We may try to control our human relationships but can we control God? Technology alters the I-Thou relationship by manipulating relatedness through an artificial medium, an arbitrary "it." In an "I-It" relation, Richard Gaillardetz writes, we objectify the world around us, placing everything into distinct categories and imposing order on our world. In the I-Thou relation, we do not seek to objectify the world, making it accessible for manipulation and control by putting people and things into their respective categories; rather, we move out to the world in a stance of attentiveness, becoming present, vulnerable, and receptive to what the world has to offer.[10]

Modern technology has reshaped our daily existence in ways that can make it difficult to experience the grace of God in our lives.[11] The loss of "feeling" at the heart of creation, we might say, is a loss of mystery at the heart of creation. Because we are no longer grasped by mystery we no longer relate to anything outside ourselves as essential to us. To stand in creation in openness to God requires a prayerful, penetrating vision. We must see things for what they are in their individual creation, each uniquely loved into being by God. Only in this way do we recognize that the other is where we encounter God and the truth of ourselves in God.

But this type of penetrating vision requires time to deepen. A technological mindset cannot comprehend that "dead time" of which modern technology tries to rid us is often the arena of grace. In her Madeleva Lecture, Kathleen Norris observed that "it always seems that just when daily life seems most unbearable...that what is inmost breaks forth, and I realize that what had seemed 'dead time' was actually a period of gestation."[12] In our feverish obsession to fill our lives with more devices that give us what we want, instantly, without effort or engagement, do we cut ourselves off from the graced dimension of ordinary life?[13]

A disengagement from the world of artificial devices and engagement with the embodied world of God's presence demands a conscious decision to waste time among the ordinary and mundane. Just as the desert fathers and mothers shaped their lives into vessels of love by fasting, we too need to undergo "cyberfasts," periods of time when all technology is turned "off." If the fundamental I-Thou relationship is changing to an I-It relationship through artificial devices, then perhaps technology is robbing us of our ability for compassion because it is robbing us of our ability to love. When we fail to love, we fail to live compassionately with the poor, creation, and the world around us. We fall into the trap of a consumer culture which instills fear and distrust and thus the need for overconsumption, regardless of the cost to others. How can we reclaim compassion as a binding force for life on earth and the sustainability of the planet? How do we reclaim community as essential to personhood?

The late Thomas Berry said that we need a new type of religious orientation which must emerge from our new story of the universe; a new revelatory experience within the evolutionary process which is from the beginning a spiritual as well as a physical process. We are born out of the Big Bang and have evolved from the stars and elements of the universe, bound together to form the persons that we are.

Berry calls the universe the "primal sacred community," and describes a new *ecozoic* age emerging based on what we now know of our universe story: (1) The universe is a communion of subjects, not a collection of objects. (2) The earth is a single reality which can exist and survive only in its integral functioning. (3) The earth is a one-time endowment; there is no second chance. (4) The human is derivative; the earth is primary. All professions must be realigned to reflect the primacy of the earth. We need new ethical principles which recognize absolute evils of *biocide*, the killing of life systems, and *geocide*, that is, the killing of the planet. Berry calls for a reorientation of religious being in the world, to shift our attention from afterlife to this life, from spirit to matter, from heaven to earth, not to merge the divine with the immanent but to see the divine in the immanent, in the earthy ordinary reality of matter.

Berry was influenced by the work of Teilhard de Chardin who said there is nothing here below that is profane. We live in a divine milieu where every creature, person, star, and grain of sand is charged with the divine. Christ penetrates all of matter because every living being bears the weight of divine love. Teilhard emphasized that the fulfillment of the universe in God lies in humankind, since we are the growing tip of evolution's direction. Thus it is important how we awaken to a new consciousness of Christ's universal presence which is discovered in one's own self-realization and full maturity in "being-with-Christ." We must seek to unite—in all aspects of our lives—with one another and with the creatures of the earth. Such union calls us out of isolated existences into community. We must slow down, discover our essential relatedness, be patient and compassionate toward all living creatures, and realize that it is a shared planet with finite resources. We are called to see and love in solidarity with all creation. Only in this way can the earth enjoy justice and peace which means right, loving relations with the natural world of God's good creation.

Compassion requires a depth of soul, a connectedness of soul to earth, an earthiness of person to person, and a flow of love from heart to heart. To evolve toward the fullness of Christ we must be able to love the weak, the unlovable, the fragile, and lame. The Body of Christ becomes one when we ourselves create bridges of love. The compassionate person walks across the bridge into the life of another saying along the way, "you are not alone, I am with you."

Meditation

Compassion is another name for community. It is the mirror of relatedness that accepts the pain and weakness of another as one's own. It is an expression of love that says "you belong to me."

For Reflection

1. Take some quiet time to reflect on your community. Who do you belong to and who belongs to you? What is the value of community in your life?

2. Volunteer in a community event that challenges you to put aside your own concerns. Take time to reflect on this experience. How did it change your perception of yourself in relation to others?

3. If you live in community (whether family or religious), try to be conscious of the needs of others and reflect on your efforts to be compassionate.

4. Pray and reflect on the words of Jesus: "For where two or three are gathered in my name, I am there among them" (Matthew 18:20).

Passion

| Compassion needs passion. It needs the fire burning within the human heart that is unafraid of life's terrors and wonders. If we lack compassion today, it is probably because we lack passion as well.

In his own day, Jesus of Nazareth was aware that religion had fallen into the hands of political zealots, and hearts once turned to God had grown cold. "I came to bring fire to the earth," he exclaimed, "and how I wish it were already kindled!" (Luke 12:49). Francis of Assisi "burned" with love for the Crucified, according to Bonaventure, and wanted to be a martyr following the footprints of Christ. Teilhard de Chardin spoke of the fire of love at the heart of the universe which he saw emanating from the sacred heart of Christ. He wrote: "In the beginning there were not coldness and darkness, there was *Fire*."[1] The French philosopher Albert Camus said we must "live to the point of tears," let life get inside and stir up the embers within. Most of us try to put fires out, however, as soon as they appear. We are afraid of fire.

There can be no compassion where there is no *eros*. "We are fired into life with a madness that comes from the gods," Ronald Rolheiser writes, "and this energy is the root of all love, hate, creativity, joy and sadness."[2] Eros is desire or the intense yearning for another. The sixth-century mystical writer Pseudo-Dionysius spoke of the whole cosmos as erotic. This may surprise us, but St. Paul described creation's longing for its fulfillment as a groaning: "We know that the whole creation has been *groaning* as in labor pains until now" (Romans 8:22). From where does this yearning arise? Dionysius said from the divine Good itself. The whole outpouring of divine love in the universe is God's yearning for the heart of matter to become love itself. The whole creation "cries out for perfection," Bonaventure said; every living being longs for its fulfillment.

This yearning of matter for spirit speaks to us of sexuality at the heart of cosmic life. Rolheiser explains that the word *sex* has a Latin root, the verb *secare*. In Latin *secare* means (literally) "to cut off," "to sever," "to amputate." To be "sexed" therefore literally means to be cut off, to be severed from, to be amputated from the whole.[3] A sexual universe is one cut off from the whole and longing for its completion. The holiness of matter is its yearning for spiritual union.

The body too is holy in its yearning for spiritual union. Yet we deny the body its voice crying out in the pain of longing, in the same way we deny matter its yearning for spiritual union. We have made passion a platonic ideal and the body an inert object of control and manipulation. We no longer recognize true passion as the stuff that the stars and moon are made of or "the Love that moves the sun and other stars," as Dante wrote.[4] The soul wanders amidst platonic ideals, and the body has become a victim of consumerism. We have lost passion because we have lost the sense of the human person as an erotic being, longing for wholeness in union with another. *Eros* has become a consumer commodity in a highly charged sexual culture. Instead of *eros* evoking the deepest desires of cosmic and human life, it has been reduced to all that is least in us. It is no wonder robot companions are on the horizon. Without the heart-filled body, we cannot love. When we lose the fire of soul within us, we lose the zest for living and become lost in a world of ideas, blind to the human person, as if ideas alone can fulfill us.

Francis was a man of passion as well as compassion. The author of the *Mirror of Perfection* states that Francis "loved fire with singular affection because of its beauty and usefulness." The story is told of how one time Francis was sitting close to a hearth and his pants caught fire. Although he felt the heat of the fire, he did not want to extinguish it. His companion wanted to extinguish the flames, but Francis told him "not to hurt Brother Fire." The brother quenched the flames with water, but he did so against Francis' will.[5] Fire was an image of Francis' life, and he burned with a deep unbridled zeal that bordered on the dramatic if not insane at times.

But Francis' fire was imbued with love. He loved deeply, especially his soul mate, Clare of Assisi. There is a story of Francis and Clare at the Porziuncula, the little church where the Franciscan movement started. The story conveys the bond of passion between the two saints who were supposedly at prayer in the Porziuncula. According to the story, the local citizens saw a great fire shooting up from the Porziuncula and ran to put out the fire. As they entered the church to quench the fire, they found the two saints rapt in contemplation, two souls bound in a single flame of love.[6]

Fire, like passion, is fearful, frightening, illuminating, and transforming. The person who fears fire probably fears passion as well. But what do we fear? Why do we lack the passion needed today to transform the world, to live courageously in love? I think we fear losing ourselves; if we throw ourselves into a fire of consuming love, nothing of us will remain. We do not *believe* in life after death. One must *believe* in a power greater than oneself at the heart of life in order to lose one's life to the fire of passion. Jesus of Nazareth was consumed by the Father's love and trusted in this love as he was betrayed in the Garden of Gethsemane. This trust reached its radical height not in the felt experience of the Father's presence but in the radical rupture of abandonment on the cross: "My God, my God, why have you forsaken me?" (Matthew 27:46) He could do no other but surrender to love, and through his death a new creation was born.

Trust in God requires not the felt experience of God but the handing over of one's life to God in darkness and silence, realizing that one's life is not one's own but belongs entirely to God. Francis *trusted* in the power of God's love present in the poor, the lepers, the sick, and the simple creatures of life. He handed himself over to this power as one completely embraced by love. Through the fire that consumed his ego, Francis gave birth to a deeper self in love; he was born anew, and this birth was a new Francis in whom was visible the face of Christ.

The Energy of Love

In the twentieth century Teilhard de Chardin spoke of harnessing the energies of love as a new discovery of fire: "The day will come when, after harnessing the ether, the winds, the tides, gravitation, we shall harness for God the energies of love. And, on that day, for the second time in the history of the world, man will have discovered fire."[7] Through the super convergence of energies, Teilhard saw the birthing of Christ, the unity of all things in love, as the goal of the universe. If we truly believe that matter is holy, then we must act to make Christ alive as oneness-in-love. Compassion is love that enkindles; it raises the dead to life and renews the power of love.

To have compassion, we must believe in the power of love. Today, the fire of compassion is weak because we do not believe that love can transform earth into heaven. Our culture is so used to the Platonic idea that heaven is a purely spiritual place that we have a strange new apocalyptic mentality in the twenty-first century: the fear that nothingness awaits us after this earthly life or that heaven is a place we must merit.

We do not believe that this earth is capable of becoming a new creation because we do not believe that this earthly creation, indeed the whole universe, is God-filled. Our love is weak and self-centered because our God is vague and abstract. Heaven is not a place of disembodied spirits but an embrace of love that transforms this present earthly life into the divine presence of enduring love. Heaven is this world clearly seen.

Compassion binds together the fragments of life, making fragments into wholes and forming new creations. Every act of love is a new beginning, a new creation. To live compassionately is to believe in a love greater than ourselves yet intimately present to us, a love visible in the trees, the streams, the clouds, the poor, nonbelievers, and all who share the life that is our life—a love binding us together without constraints. We must believe that each person is capable of being transformed by love, that each tree, flower, animal, living creature, the stones, the sand, the sky—everything is capable of being transformed by love. And that when all is united by a luminous thread of love, Christ will be visible in the universe.

In the popular book *Tuesdays with Morrie,* author Mitch Albom tells of his reunion with his sociology professor after seeing him on television speaking about his battle with Lou Gehrig's disease. Mitch contacts his beloved professor and travels from his home in Detroit to Professor Morrie's home in West Newton, Massachusetts. Teacher and student reunite, and Mitch begins visiting his professor every Tuesday, caring for him and listening to his insights on life. Their meetings become a celebration of life, friendship, and family. Morrie advises Mitch to reject the popular culture based on greed, selfishness, and superficiality and create his own culture founded on love, acceptance, and human goodness, a culture that upholds a set of ethical values that promote life. The power of Morrie's feeble life to transform the life of his student is a powerful example of compassion and conversion. After Morrie's death, Mitch reunites with his estranged brother who is suffering from cancer. He has learned the greatest lesson of life—that love is stronger than death.

Lessons From Science

As human beings and societies we seem separate, but in our roots we are part of an indivisible whole and share in the same cosmic process. Each relatively autonomous and stable structure is to be understood not as something independent and permanently existent but rather as a product that has been formed in the whole flowing movement.[8] Relatedness prevails over autonomy when the welfare of another is more important than the welfare of oneself; a consciousness of immanent relatedness. Francis felt the sufferings of the poor as his own, and he loved the poor as the very image of Christ. His world was much larger than himself because it was rooted in divine love. He *believed* God was fully present, intimately united to weak, fragile flesh and that all created life was capable of glorifying God in its present reality. He believed compassion could transform earth into heaven, and this earth-transformed-into heaven would be the Body of Christ.

In discussing the role of the human person in creation, Bonaventure said that the human is one who shares in the materiality of the world through the body and possesses an intelligent, spiritual nature that is open to union with God. The way we relate to God and one another has profound effects; our actions influence the whole creation. When *eros* finds its fruitful aim, it can set the world on fire. One has only to reflect in our own time on the *eros* of Mahatma Gandhi, Martin Luther King, or Mother Teresa.

Similarly, compassion ignited by *eros* has the power to transform hearts of stone into hearts of flesh. We have the power to help create a world of peace. We have the power to heal divisions, bind up wounds, and gladden human hearts. We have the power to create a sustainable earth, but do we have the passion to do so? We are to love because love unites; love is the fire that moves the heart of evolution.

We cannot substitute the human face for an idea or a number. We cannot replace meadows and fields with strip malls without destroying community. We cannot consume any living thing without bearing the cost of our actions and weighing the cost of love. We must begin to love in a new way. We need a new beginning of compassion. John O'Donohue writes: "Sometimes the greatest challenge is to actually begin; there is something deep in us that conspires with what wants to remain within safe boundaries and stay the same."[9] We must place profound trust in the act of beginning. "There can be no growth if we do not remain open and vulnerable to what is new and different."[10] Earth is a community dying to live and every single human person is dying to love. If we fail to love anew, to build the earth, then we will bear its revolt, as Bonaventure wrote:

> Therefore, any person who is not illumined by such great splendors in created things is blind. Anyone who is not

awakened by such great outcries is deaf. Anyone who is not led by such effects to give praise to God is mute. Anyone who does not turn to the First Principle as a result of such signs is a fool. Therefore open your eyes; alert your spiritual ears; unlock your lips, and apply your heart so that in all creatures you may see, hear, praise, love, and adore, magnify, and honor your God lest the entire world rise up against you.[11]

Meditation

Compassion is the spirit of love that unites where there are broken hearts; the power to transform hearts of stone into hearts of flesh.

For Reflection

1. Take some time to reflect on what you are passionate about. Write down your experience of this passion. Then reflect on areas of your life that lack passion. Write down the difficulties of these areas. In what ways can you redirect your life's *eros*?

2. Consider the words of Jesus: "I have come to bring fire on the earth, and how I wish it were already kindled" (Luke 12:49). What speaks to you in this passage? As a disciple of Jesus, what fire are you bringing upon the earth?

3. Reflect on the relationship between passion and compassion. Are these related in your life?

4. Reflect on times in your life when you experienced suffering. Did this suffering open you to love or cause you to withdraw into yourself? Can you see the bond between suffering and love?

5. Clare of Assisi was inspired by the Lamentation "Look and see if there are any sorrow like my sorrow" (1:12). She used it when praying before the mirror of the cross. How does this Lamentation

speak to you? Where are you in the Passion of Christ and where do you see God?

| There is a story Jesus tells us in the Gospel of Luke that embraces the meaning of compassion as I have tried to explore it here. In the parable a priest and a Levite pass by a victim abandoned at the side of the road. They each see him, but neither one is moved to help; instead each one passes by to the other side of the road to avoid contact with the victim (cf. Luke 10:31, 32). A Samaritan, however, passing by sees the victim not as an impediment to his journey or a curiosity but as one who needs his help (cf. Luke 10:33). The compassion of the Samaritan is not a fleeting sentimentality but a profound emergence of care from identifying with the other, a "seeing" that moves him to identification. Howard Grey explains:

> Compassion is an affective identification with the human situation of the other, here in all the victim's pain and abandonment, vulnerability and humiliation; it is to recognize the solidarity within human suffering and pain. Compassion comes from a welcoming heart; it does not come from command and it must be wary of manipulation and trickery. This is precisely why the parable is so artful. The victim does not dramatize his plight, he simply *is* his plight. The Samaritan offers himself to the victim as one co-responsible for his plight. He does not give the victim "things"; he does not do *for* the victim. Rather the Samaritan gives what are symbols of his own humanity: his presence ("he went to him"); his

very clothing ("he bandaged his wounds," implying that the
Samaritan tore his own clothing to make the bandages);
his supplies ("having poured oil and wine on them" [the
wounds]); his physical exertions, time, and monies ("he put
him on his own animal, brought him to an inn, and took care
of him"). In these actions, the Samaritan has not so much
discovered the stranger but made the stranger his concern
and responsibility. He does not simply serve the victim but
brings the victim into his life. The Samaritan merges his life
and that of the wounded stranger.[1]

Where are we in this story of the Good Samaritan? On which side
of the road do we travel? Francis of Assisi was once the Levite who
passed by the victims of suffering, the lepers, and then he crossed the
road to become not only the Good Samaritan but the leper himself.
In Francis, the Good Samaritan and the leper became one.

It was not an easy crossing, and Francis had to persevere through
the difficulties of conversion, of turning from his self-centeredness
toward God-centeredness. What made possible his turning was
meeting God in the crucified Christ. He saw that God appears in
what is weak and fragile and rejected by many. He came to know this
God of humble love within himself. God loved him and embraced
him despite his own brokenness. To know God within oneself is the
starting point for knowing God in others, in their true being. There is
no God "out there" who is not first within the human heart.

As Francis came to know God more deeply through prayer, meditation, and long periods of solitude, he came to see that he was not
alone in this world; he was created by God and in God his life had
meaning and purpose. Coming to this knowledge allowed him to
loosen the reigns of control on his life; he was at home in his own skin

and being at home within himself he could open himself up to love. Compassion blossomed in Francis' life like a seed on newly tilled soil. Love softened his heart to feel the pain of others whose pain became his own, in the same way that our pain belongs to God. He showed patience and kindness to those suffering because he felt something of his own suffering in theirs.

Compassion is realized when we know ourselves related to one another, a deep relatedness of our humanity despite our limitations. It goes beyond the differences that separate us and enters the shared space of created being. To enter this space is to have space within ourselves, to welcome into our lives the stranger, the outcast, and the poor. Love is stronger than death and the heart that no longer fears death is truly free. Compassion flourishes when we have nothing to protect and everything to share. It is the gravity of all living beings that binds together all that is weak and limited into a single ocean of love.

We have the capacity to heal this earth of its divisions, its wars, its violence, and its hatreds. This capacity is the love within us to suffer with another and to love the other without reward. Love that transcends the ego is love that heals. When we lose ourselves for the sake of love, we shall find ourselves capable of real love. Compassion flows best from a heart open, free, and deeply in love with life. It rises above the individual and yearns for oneness of heart.

Compassion knows no other language than the language of love. Let us learn this language and speak it aloud with our hands, our feet, and our eyes, for compassion can birth the new creation.

Closing Prayer

God of overflowing goodness, since time began you have been
revealing yourself in all creation. From the Big Bang to the convergence
of galaxies, from the distant stars to this Earth, which is our
home, you have never ceased shaping and fashioning us, urging us
toward life. We are truly amazed at the work of your hands and for
the life of Jesus, who reflects your radiance. We are blessed by the gift
of self-awareness that you have given to us. Help us to be mindful
that we are the universe conscious of itself and that we are sister and
brother to all creation. Open our hearts to receive the gift of life that
comes to us each day from the sun, the stars, plant life, animal life,
and the unique giftedness of each human person. Lead us kindly on
this cosmic journey that we may become the fullness of Christ who
is our peace. Amen.

Acknowledgments

1. Donald P. McNeill, Douglas A. Morrison, and Henri J. M. Nouwen, *Compassion: A Reflection on the Christian Life* (New York: Doubleday, 1982), p. 4.

Chapter One

1. Paul M. Allen and Joan deRis Allen, *Francis of Assisi's Canticle of the Creatures: A Modern Spiritual Path* (New York: Continuum, 1996), p. 45.

2. Thomas of Celano, "The Life of Saint Francis," in *Francis of Assisi: Early Documents*, vol. 1, *The Saint,* Regis J. Armstrong, J. A. Wayne Hellmann, and William J. Short, eds. (New York: New City Press, 1999), pp. 183–184. Hereafter referred to as *FA:ED* followed by volume and page number.

3. Thomas of Celano, "The Life of Saint Francis," in *FA:ED* I, pp. 184–185.

4. Thomas of Celano, "The Life of Saint Francis," in *FA:ED* I, p. 187.

5. Thomas of Celano, "Remembrance of the Desire of a Soul," in *Francis of Assisi: Early Documents*, vol. 2, *The Founder,* Regis J. Armstrong, J. A. Wayne Hellmann, and William J. Short, eds. (New York: New City Press, 2000), p. 249.

6. Francis of Assisi, "Testament," 3 in *FA:ED* I, p. 124.

7. Catherine de Vinck, *A Basket of Bread: An Anthology of Selected Poems* (New York: Alba House, 1996), pp. 6–7.

8. James Jeans, *The Mysterious Universe* (New York: Macmillan, 1931), p. 158, cited in Lothar Schäfer, "Quantum Reality, the Emergence of Complex Order from Virtual States, and the Importance of Consciousness in the Universe," *Zygon: Journal of Religion and Science* 41.3 (2006), p. 509.

9. Lester K. Little, *Religious Poverty and the Profit Economy in Medieval Europe* (New York: Cornell University Press, 1978), p. 341.

10. Thomas of Celano, "The Remembrance of the Desire of a Soul," LXI.95 in *Francis of Assisi: Early Documents*, vol. II, *The Founder*, Regis J. Armstrong, J.A. Wayne Hellmann, and William J. Short, eds. (New York: New City Press, 2000), p. 310.

11. See Sally McFague, *The Body of God: An Ecological Theology* (Minneapolis: Augsburg, 1993).

12. Thomas of Celano, "The Remembrance of the Desire of a Soul," V in *FA:ED* II, p. 248.

13. Thomas of Celano, "The Remembrance of the Desire of a Soul," V.9-10 in *FA:ED* II, p. 249.

14. Francis of Assisi, "Testament," 3 in *FA:ED* I, p. 124.

15. Thomas of Celano, "The Remembrance of the Desire of a Soul," VI.10 in *FA:ED* II, p. 249.

16. Francis of Assisi, "Testament," 3 in *FA:ED* I, p. 124.

Chapter Two

1. Francis of Assisi, "The Prayer Before the Crucifix," in *FA:ED* I, p. 40.

2. Michael Blastic, "Contemplation and Compassion: A Franciscan Ministerial Spirituality" in *Franciscan Leadership in Ministry: Foundations in History, Theology, and Spirituality*, vol. 7, *Spirit and Life: A Journal of Contemporary Franciscanism*, Anthony Carrozzo,

Vincent Cushing, and Kenneth Himes, eds. (New York: The Franciscan Institute, 1997), p. 154.

3. *The Confessions of St. Augustine*, John K. Ryan, trans.(New York: Doubleday, 1960), p. 84.

4. Pierre Teilhard de Chardin, *The Divine Milieu: An Essay on the Interior Life*, William Collins, trans. (New York: Harper & Row, 1960), p. 115.

5. Oliver Clément, *The Roots of Christian Mysticism* (Hyde Park, N.Y.: New City Press, 1993), p. 76.

6. Clément, *Roots of Christian Mysticism*, p. 87.

7. Francis of Assisi, "The Office of the Passion," "Psalm VII.8," in *FA:ED* I, p. 147.

8. Vladimir Lossky, *Orthodox Theology: An Introduction*, Ian and Ihita Kesarcodi-Watson, trans. (Crestwoood, N.Y.: St. Vladimir's Seminary Press, 1978), p. 73.

9. Alice Walker, *The Color Purple* (New York: Washington Square Press, 1992), pp. 177–179.

10. Cited in Richard Kearney, *Anatheism* (New York: Columbia University Press, 2010), p. 41.

11. Kearney, *Anatheism*, p. 69.

12. Thomas of Celano, "The Remembrance of the Desire of a Soul," LXI.95 in *FA:ED* II, p. 309.

13. Thomas of Celano, "The Remembrance of the Desire of a Soul," VI.11 in *FA:ED* II, p. 250.

14. Roberta C. Bondi, "Christianity and Cultural Diversity I. The Spirituality of Syriac-Speaking Christians," in *World Spirituality: Origins to the Twelfth Century*, Bernard McGinn, John Meyendorff, and Jean Leclercq, eds. vol. 16, *World Spirituality: An Encyclopedic History of the Religious Quest*, Ewert Cousins, ed. (New York: Crossroad, 1987), pp. 152–161.

15. Bonaventure, "The Major Legend of Saint Francis" 1.6 in *FA:ED* II, p. 534.

16. *The Assisi Compilation*, 34 in *FA:ED* II, p. 140.

Chapter Three

1. Ewert H. Cousins, *Christ of the 21ˢᵗ Century* (Rockport, Mass.: Element Books, 1992), p. 6; "Teilhard's Concept of Religion and the Religious Phenomenon of Our Time," *Teilhard Studies* Number 49 (Fall 2004), pp. 10–11.

2. Bonaventure, *Soliloquium* 2.12 (VIII, 49). Zachary Hayes, trans., *Bonaventure: Mystical Writings* (New York: Crossroad, 1999), p. 140. Bonaventure writes: "O my soul, I think that you exist more truly where you love than where you merely live, since you are transformed into the likeness of whatever you love, through the power of this love itself."

3. Thomas Merton, *Conjectures of a Guilty Bystander* (Garden City, N.Y.: Doubleday, 1966), pp. 140–142.

Chapter Four

1. Cited in Kenneth and Michael Himes, "Creation and an Environmental Ethic," in *Fullness of Faith: The Public Significance of Theology* (New York: Paulist, 1993), p. 119.

2. Himes, p. 119.

3. Himes, p. 119.

4. Himes, p. 119.

5. Michael Himes and Kenneth J. Himes, "The Sacrament of Creation: Toward an Environmental Theology," *Commonweal* (Jan. 26 1990), p. 45.

6. The basis of this section is Regis Armstrong's discussion on poverty in Francis of Assisi in *Francis of Assisi: Writings for a Gospel*

Life (New York: Crossroad, 1994), pp. 152–165. See especially p. 154.

7. Francis of Assisi, "Admonition VII," in *FA:ED* I, p. 132.

8. Cited in Henri J. M. Nouwen, *The Wounded Healer: Ministry in Contemporary Society* (New York: Image, 1979), p. 91.

9. In his "Earlier Rule," Francis writes, "Let the brothers be careful not to slander or engage in disputes…let them not quarrel among themselves…let them love one another…let them not grumble… let them not consider the least sins of others." See "Earlier Rule" 11 in *FA:ED* I, p. 72. See also Admonitions 8, 14. In Admonition VIII Francis says, "Whoever envies his brother the good that the Lord says or does in him incurs a sin of blasphemy because he envies the Most High himself who ways and does every good thing" (*FA:ED* I, p. 132).

10. Francis of Assisi, "Admonition XIV," in *FA:ED* I, p. 133.

11. Johannes Metz, *Poverty of Spirit* (New York: Newman, 1960), p. 45 cited in Nouwen, *Reaching Out: The Three Movements of Spiritual Life*, p. 107.

12. Thomas Merton, *New Seeds of Contemplation* (New York: New Directions, 1961), p. 189.

13. Barbara Fiand, *Living the Vision: Religious Vows in an Age of Change* (New York: Crossroad, 1990), p. 59.

14. Francis of Assisi, "Letter to a Minister," in *FA:ED* I, pp. 97–98.

Chapter Five

1. I am indebted to Fr. Adolpho Nicholas, S.J. for this phrase.

2. Cited in Joyce Rupp, *The Cup of Our Life: A Guide for Spiritual Growth* (Notre Dame, Ind.: Ave Maria, 1997), p. 110.

3. Hans Urs von Balthasar, *The Glory of the Lord: Theological Aesthetics*, Andrew Louth, Francis McDonagh, and Brian McNeil, trans., vol. 2, *Studies in Theological Style: Clerical Styles*, Joseph Fessio, ed. (San Francisco: Ignatius, 1984), p. 353.

4. Von Balthasar, *Glory of the Lord*, p. 356.

5. Francis of Assisi, "A Letter to the Entire Order" in *FA:ED* Vol I. p. 118.

6. Elizabeth of the Trinity, *The Complete Works*, vol. 1, *General Introduction: Major Spiritual Writings* (Washington, D.C.: ICS, 1984), p. 179.

7. Leonard Lehman, "Francis' 'Office of the Passion,'" *Greyfriars Review* 12 (1998), pp. 143–168.

8. René Girard, *The Scapegoat*, Yvonne Freccero, trans. (Baltimore: Johns Hopkins University Press, 1986), p. 102.

9. Girard, *The Scapegoat*, p. 104.

10. Francis of Assisi, "Office of the Passion," I.7 in *FA:ED* I, p. 140.

11. Francis of Assisi, "Office of the Passion," II.10 in *FA:ED* I, p. 142.

12. Francis of Assisi, "Office of the Passion," IV.6–7 in *FA:ED* I, p. 144.

13. Francis of Assisi, "Office of the Passion," VI.7 in *FA:ED* I, p. 144.

14. Girard, *The Scapegoat*, p. 41. The mention of the late-medieval chronicler, Guillaume de Machaut, refers to the first chapter of *The Scapegoat*, "Guillaume de Machaut and the Jews," in which Girard analyzes Guillaume's claim and the widely held belief of the period that the Jews were responsible for the Black Death.

15. "The Assisi Compilation," 78 in *FA:ED* II, p. 180.

16. Thomas of Celano, "The Remembrance of the Desire of a Soul," LXXXVII.124 in *FA:ED* II, p. 329.

17. Thomas of Celano, "The Remembrance of the Desire of a Soul," CXXXIV.177 in *FA:ED* II, p. 360.

18. Thomas of Celano, "The Remembrance of the Desire of a Soul," CXLII.190 in *FA:ED* II, p. 369.

19. Thomas of Celano, "The Remembrance of the Desire of a Soul," CXLII.190 in *FA:ED* II, p. 369.

20. Thomas of Celano, "The Remembrance of the Desire of a Soul," CXLII.190 in *FA:ED* II, p. 369.

21. "The Little Flowers of Saint Francis," ch. 26 in *Francis of Assisi: Early Documents*, vol. 3, *The Prophet*, Regis J. Armstrong, J.A. Wayne Hellmann, and William J. Short, eds. (New York: New City Press, 2001), pp. 610–611.

22. Michael Blastic, "Attentive Compassion: Franciscan Resources for Ministry," in *Handbook of Spirituality for Ministers*, Vol. 2, *Perspectives for the 21st Century*, Robert J. Wicks, ed. (New York: Paulist, 2000), p. 255.

23. Graziano Marechesi, "Tabernacles," in *Wheat and Weeds and the Wolf of Gubbio* (Kansas City: Sheed & Ward, 1994), pp. 5–7; Dawn Nothwehr, *The Franciscan View of the Human Person: Some Central Elements*, The Franciscan Heritage Series, Vol. 3, Joseph P. Chinnici, ed. (St. Bonaventure, N.Y.: Franciscan Institute Publications, 2005), pp. 67–68.

24. Nothwehr, p. 69.

25. Nothwehr, p. 69.

Chapter Six

1. John O'Donohue, *To Bless the Space Between Us: A Book of Blessings* (New York: Doubleday, 2008), p. 97.

2. Bonaventure, "The Major Legend of Saint Francis," 13.3 in *FA:ED* II, p. 632.

3. Richard Rohr, "Contemplation and Compassion: The Second Gaze," *Radical Grace* 18.6 (November–December 2005). http://www.cacradicalgrace.org/resources/rg/novdec.

4. Rohr.

5. McNeill et al., *Compassion*, p. 18.

6. Henri J. M. Nouwen, *Reaching Out: The Three Movements of the Spiritual Life* (New York: Doubleday, 1966), p. 74.

7. Nouwen, p. 74.

8. Francis of Assisi, "Office of the Passion," in *FA:ED* I, pp. 146–147.

Chapter Seven

1. Bonaventure, "Major Legend of Saint Francis," 9.1 in *FA:ED* II, p. 596.

2. Jim Edmiston, "How to Love a Worm? Biodiversity: Franciscan Spirituality and Praxis," in *Franciscan Theology of the Environment: An Introductory Reader*, Dawn Nothwehr, ed. (Quincy, Ill.: Franciscan Press, 2002), p. 388.

3. See Gregory Bateson, *Mind and Nature: A Necessary Unity* (New York: E. P. Dutton, 1979); Peter Harries-Jones, *A Recursive Vision: Ecological Understanding and Gregory Bateson* (Toronto: University of Toronto Press, 2002).

4. Emmanuel Falque, "The Phenomenological Act of *Perscrutatio* in the Proemium of St. Bonaventure's Commentary on the Sentences," Elisa Mangina, trans. *Medieval Philosophy and Theology* 10 (2001), p. 9.

5. Falque, "Phenomenological Act of *Perscrutatio*," p. 11.

6. Falque, "Phenomenological Act of *Perscrutatio*," p. 12.

7. Falque, "Phenomenological Act of *Perscrutatio*," p. 13.

8. Falque, "Phenomenological Act of *Perscrutatio*," p. 18.

9. Bonaventure *Breviloquium* 1.8 (V, 216). The critical edition of Bonaventure's works is the *Opera Omnia* ed. PP. Collegii S. Bonaventurae, 10 vols. (Quaracchi, 1882–1902). Latin texts are indicated by volume and page number in parentheses.

10. At the conclusion of his *Lignum vitae* Bonaventure prays for the seven gifts of the Holy Spirit, beginning with the gift of wisdom. The prayer is addressed *to* the "most kind Father" *through* "his only-begotten Son, who for us became man, was crucified and glorified," *for* "the Spirit of sevenfold grace who rested upon you in all fullness." Bonaventure therefore affirms the crucified Christ as the *totum integrale* of theology and wisdom as the highest gift of the Spirit by which "we may taste the life-giving flavors of the fruit of the tree of life, which You truly are." See Ewert H. Cousins, *Bonaventure: The Soul's Journey into God, The Tree of Life, The Life of St. Francis* (New York: Paulist, 1978), p. 174.

11. For a more detailed discussion on the types and properties of wisdom see Christopher Cullen, *Bonaventure* (New York: Oxford University Press, 2006), pp. 23–35; Gregory LaNave, *Through Holiness to Wisdom: The Nature of Theology according to St. Bonaventure* (Roma: Instituto Storico Dei Cappuccini, 2005), pp. 147–192.

12. Bonaventure *Collationes in Hexaëmeron (Hex.)* 2. 28 (V, 340–341). José de Vinck, Engl. trans., "Collations on the Six Days," in *Works of St. Bonaventure*, vol. V (Paterson, N.J.: St. Anthony Guild Press, 1970), p. 35.

13. *Hex.* 2.30 (V, 341). De Vinck, *Collations on Six Days*, pp. 36–37.

14. *Hex.* 2.31 (V, 341). De Vinck, *Collations on Six Days*, p. 37.

15. *Hex.* 2.32 (V, 342). De Vinck, *Collations on Six Days*, p. 39.

16. Thomas of Celano, "Remembrance of the Desire of a Soul," LXVIII, *FA:ED* II, p. 314.

17. Bonaventure, "Major Legend of Saint Francis," 8.6 in *FA:ED* II, p. 590.

18. Thomas of Celano, "The Life of Saint Francis," in *FA:ED* I, pp. 250–51.

19. Thomas of Celano, "Remembrance of the Desire of a Soul," in *FA:ED* II, p. 354.

20. Although there is no specific mention of Jesus Christ in this hymn, the brother-sister relationships that Francis describes echo his sense of family relationships in his "Later Version of the Letter to the Faithful" where he writes: "We are spouses when the faithful soul is joined to Jesus Christ by the Holy Spirit. We are brothers when we do the will of his Father who is in heaven. We are mothers when we carry Him in our heart and body through love and a pure and sincere conscience; we give birth to Him through His holy manner of working, which should shine before others as an example." See *Francis of Assisi*, "Later Admonition and Exhortation," in *FA:ED* I, p. 49. Familial relationships for Francis are grounded in the Trinity and the integral relationship between the Trinity and Christ. A Trinitarian theology with Christ as center seems to underlie his *Canticle of the Creatures*.

21. Susanna Peters Coy, "The Problem of 'Per' in the *Cantico di frate sole* of Saint Francis," *Modern Language Notes* 91 (1976), pp. 1–11.

22. Francis of Assisi, "The Canticle of Creatures," in *FA:ED* I, pp. 113–114.

23. Eloi Leclerc, *The Canticle of Creatures: Symbols of Union*, Matthew J. O'Connell, trans. (Chicago: Franciscan Herald, 1970), p. 222.

24. Leonard Lehmann, *Tiefe und Weite: Der universale Grundzug in den Gebeten des Franziskus von Assisi* (Werl: Dietrich-Coelde-Verlag, 1984), p. 312.

25. Kenan B. Osborne, *The Franciscan Intellectual Tradition: Tracing its Origins and Identifying its Central Components*, Elise Saggau, ed., vol. 1, *The Heritage Series*, Joseph P. Chinnici, ed. (New York: Franciscan Institute Publications, 2001), p. 42.

26. Ilia Delio, "The *Canticle of Brother Sun:* A Song of Christ Mysticism," *Franciscan Studies* 52 (1992), p. 20.

Chapter Eight

1. Noreen Herzfeld, *In Our Image: Artificial Intelligence and the Human Spirit* (Minneapolis: Augsburg Fortress, 2002), p. 9.

2. Herzfeld, p. 9.

3. Anne Kull, "Speaking Cyborg: Technoculture and Technonature," *Zygon* 37.2 (June 2002), p. 283.

4. Philip Hefner, *Technology and Human Becoming* (Minneapolis: Fortress, 2003), p. 75. Hefner notes that "technosapien" is a more recent coinage that aims at the same idea as "cyborg." Some futurists now speak of "cyber sapiens" saying "we will no longer be Homo sapiens, but Cyber sapiens—a creature part digital and part biological that will have placed more distance between its DNA and the destinies they force upon us than any other animal...a creature capable of steering our own evolution." See KurzweilAI.net.

5. For example see Naomi Goldenberg, *Returning Words to Flesh: Feminism, Psychoanalysis, and the Resurrection of the Body* (Boston: Beacon, 1990).

6. See, for example, the work of Robert Geraci who discusses machine apotheosis and the challenge to Christian theologies today. Robert M. Geraci, "Robots and the Sacred in Science and Science Fiction: Theological Implications of Artificial Intelligence," *Zygon* 42.4 (December 2007), pp. 961–980; Geraci, "Spiritual Robots: Religion and Our Scientific View of the Natural World," *Theology and Science* 4.3 (2006), pp. 229–246.

7. See RobotWorx http://www.robots.com/applications.php?app= machine+loading.

8. Cited in Theodore Roszak, "Evolution and the Transcendence of Mind," *Perspectives* 1.2 (May 15, 1996) http://www.mentalhelp. net/poc/view_doc.php?type=doc&id=274.

9. N. Katherine Hayles, *How We Became Posthuman: Virtual Bodies in Cybernetics, Literature, and Informatics* (Chicago: University of Chicago Press, 1999), pp. 2–3.

10. Hayles, pp. 2–3.

11. Ray Kurzweil defines the singularity as the point at which machines become sufficiently intelligent to start teaching themselves. When that happens, he indicates, the world will irrevocably shift from the biological to the mechanical. See Ray Kurzweil, *The Age of Spiritual Machines: When Computers Exceed Human Intelligence* (New York: Viking, 1999), pp. 3–5.

12. Geraci, "Spiritual Robots," p. 235.

13. See Hans Moravec, *Mind Children: The Future of Robot and Human Intelligence* (Cambridge, Mass.: Harvard University Press, 1990).

14. Daniel Crevier, *AI: The Tumultuous History of the Search for Artificial Intelligence* (New York: Basic, 1994), pp. 278–280.

15. Cited in Stephen Garner, "Praying with Machines: religious dreaming in cyberspace," *Stimulus* 12. 3 (2004), p. 20.

16. Garner, p. 20.

17. Garner, p. 20; D.O. Berger, "Cybergnosticism: Or, Who Needs a Body Anyway?" *Concordia Journal* 25 (1999), pp. 340–345.

18. Michael Heim, *The Metaphysics of Virtual Reality* (New York: Oxford University Press, 1993), p. 89, cited in Garner, "Praying with Machines," p. 20.

19. Hans Moravec, *Robot: Mere Machine to Transcendent Mind* (New York: Oxford University, 1999), pp. 143ff.

20. Ronald Cole-Turner, "Biotechnology and the Religion-Science Discussion," in *The Oxford Handbook of Religion and Science*, Philip Clayton and Zachary Simpson, eds. (New York: Oxford University Press, 2006), p. 941.

21. Cole-Turner, p. 941.

22. Thomas of Celano, "Remembrance of the Desire of a Soul," CXXXIII in *FA:ED* II, p. 359.

23. Richard Louv, *Last Child in the Woods* (Chapel Hill, N.C.: Algonquin, 2005), p. 7.

24. Louv, p. 7.

25. Alfred Kracher, "The Diversity of Environments: Nature and Technology as Competing Myths," in *Creation's Diversity: Voices from Theology and Science*, Willem B. Drees, Hubert Meisinger, and Taede A. Smedes, eds. (New York: T&T Clark, 2008), p. 83.

26. Herzfeld, *Technology and Religion*, p. 74. Herzfeld writes: "Immersion in cyberspace sets up a cybernetic loop between the human and the machine, a loop that allows each to be changed by the others. The player becomes the game, and the game plays the player."

27. O'Donohue, p. 49.

Chapter Nine

1. For a discussion on Gaia see James Lovelock, *Gaia: A New Look at Life on Earth* (New York: Oxford University Press, 2000).
2. Tijn Touber, "Do Primates Feel Compassion?" http://www.care2. com/greenliving/do-primates-feel-compassion.html#.
3. Touber.
4. Thomas of Celano, "Remembrance of the Desire of a Soul," *CXXII.* 165 in *FA:ED* II, pp. 353–354.
5. "Assisi Compilation 93" in *FA:ED* II, p. 196.
6. Charles Eisenstein, "A Circle of Gifts," http://shareable.net/ blog/a-circle-of-gifts.
7. Raimon Panikkar, "The End of History: The Threefold Structure of Human Time-Consciousness," in *Teilhard and the Unity of Knowledge*, Thomas M. King and James F. Salmon, eds. (New York: Paulist, 1983), p. 108.
8. Dacher Keltner, "The Compassionate Instinct," *Greater Good: Science of Meaningful Life* (Spring 2004) http://greatergood. berkeley.edu/article/item/the _compassionate_instinct/#.
9. Howard Rheingold, *Virtual Community: Homesteading on the Electronic Frontier* (Reading, Mass.: Addison-Wesley, 1993), p. 3.
10. Richard R. Gaillardetz, *Transforming Our Days: Finding God Amidst the Noise of Modern Life* (New York: Crossroad, 2000), p. 57.
11. Gaillardetz, p. 11.
12. Kathleen Norris, *The Quotidian Mysteries: Laundry, Liturgy and "Women's Work"* (New York: Paulist, 1998), p. 10.
13. Gaillardetz, p. 67.

Chapter Ten

1. Thomas King, *Teilhard's Mass: Approaches to "The Mass on the World"* (Mahwah, N.J.: Paulist, 2005), p. 147.

2. Ronald Rolheiser, *The Holy Longing: The Search for a Christian Spirituality* (New York: Doubleday, 1999), p. 192.

3. Rolheiser, *Holy Longing*, p. 193.

4. Dante Alighieri, "Canto XXXIII.145," cited in Helen M. Luke, *Dark Wood to White Rose: Journey and Transformation in Dante's Divine Comedy* (New York: Parabola, 1989), p. 199.

5. "The Beginning of a Mirror of Perfection of the Status of a Lesser Brother (the Sabatier Edition)" in *FA:ED* III, p. 365.

6. "The Little Flowers of Saint Francis," ch. 15 in *FA:ED* III, p. 591.

7. Pierre Teilhard de Chardin, *Toward the Future*, René Hague, trans. (New York: Harcourt, 1973), pp. 86–87.

8. Sharpe, "Relating the Physics and Metaphysics of David Bohm," http://www.ksharpe.com/Word/BM05.htm.

9. O'Donohue, p. 3.

10. O'Donohue, p. 2.

11. Bonaventure, *Itinerarium Mentis in Deum* 1.15. Zachary Hayes, trans., *Itinerarium Mentis in Deum*, vol. II, *Works of St. Bonaventure*, Philotheus Boehner and Zachary Hayes, eds. (St. Bonaventure, N. Y.: Franciscan Institute Publications, 2002), p. 61.

Conclusion

1. Howard Grey, "Putting the Human Back into Transhumanism," pp. 5–6. Unpublished paper for the Transhumanism Research project, Woodstock Theological Center, Georgetown University.

About the Author

Ilia Delio, O.S.F., is a key writer in the Franciscan intellectual tradition and a recognized spiritual voice today as one who can illumine critical aspects of our Catholic Christian faith, using her scholarship as a foundation for her insights. She is a senior fellow at Woodstock Theological Center, Georgetown University, where she concentrates on the areas of science and religion. She is currently involved in research projects on transhumanism, technology and evolution, and ecology and education. In 2000 she received a Templeton course award in science and religion. She is the author of numerous books, including, *Franciscan Prayer*, *The Humility of God: A Franciscan Perspective*, and *Care for Creation: A Franciscan Spirituality of the Earth*, (with Keith Douglass Warner, O.F.M., and Pamela Wood), which won two Catholic Press Book Awards in 2009.